TWEAK IT

SMALL CHANGES, BIG IMPACT

MAKE WHAT MATTERS TO YOU
HAPPEN EVERY DAY

CALI WILLIAMS YOST

CENTER
STREET

New York Boston Nashville

Copyright © 2013 by Work+Life Fit, Inc.

"Tweaks of the Week" is a registered trademark owned by the author.

Center Street
Hachette Book Group
237 Park Avenue
New York, NY 10017

www.centerstreet.com

Printed in the United States of America

RRD-C

First Edition: January 2013
10   9   8   7   6   5   4   3   2   1

Center Street is a division of Hachette Book Group, Inc.
The Center Street name and logo are trademarks of Hachette Book Group, Inc.

The Hachette Speakers Bureau provides a wide range of authors for speaking events. To find out more, go to www.hachettespeakersbureau.com or call (866) 376-6591.

The publisher is not responsible for websites (or their content) that are not owned by the publisher.

Library of Congress Cataloging-in-Publication Data
Yost, Cali Williams.
   Tweak it: small changes, big impact; make what matters to you happen
every day / Cali Williams Yost.—1st ed.
      p. cm.
   ISBN 978-0-89296-880-0 (hardcover)—ISBN 978-1-4555-1786-2 (ebook)
   1. Work-life balance.   2. Work and family.   3. Time management.   4. Quality of life.
I. Title.
   HD4904.25.Y67 2013
   650.1'1—dc23
                                                                                  2012029791

*For Andy, Emma, Maddie, and everyone who shared
their work+life "fit" stories with me over the past seventeen years.
You are my inspiration.*

Contents

Introduction

Seven Modern Truths about Work and Life

> Learn to live small and you will discover great pleasures. You will accomplish more in your life than you could ever predict if you were overly ambitious.
>
> —Thomas Moore

Work and life. As recently as twenty years ago, the rules that we all followed about when to work and when to manage everything else in life were pretty clear. Then the boundaries began to blur and the rules started to change. Unfortunately, someone forgot to send the memo with the new guidelines. Every day, we struggled to answer questions like:

Do I:
- leave work a few minutes early to get to the gym, or prepare for a meeting?
- work from home in the evening to catch up on e-mails, or meet a friend for coffee?
- cover a coworker's shift, or shop for food for the week?
- ask for overtime, or take my mother to the doctor?
- catch up on paperwork, or read at my child's school?
- go to a lunchtime networking event, or balance my checkbook?

What if I told you there was a better way? The *Tweak It* practice outlined in this book will make what matters to you happen. This simple weekly routine of small, deliberate choices, or "tweaks," will build the foundation of contentment, well-being, and order you crave, one step at a time. Imagine, if over one year, you managed to do your job but also:

- enjoyed lunches and a cup of coffee with your friends;
- updated your online professional profile on LinkedIn and attended a few networking events;
- kept track of your checking account and credit card purchases;
- took each of your kids to lunch or the movies one-on-one;
- made sure your backup child care for the summer was in place *before* the last day of school;
- completed an online course to learn a new skill for your job;
- sent out presents and birthday cards on time;
- ate mostly healthy, simple meals;
- had a few date nights with your spouse or partner;
- made it to your annual physical;
- had your car serviced so it didn't break down from preventable problems and require costly repairs;
- took a walk with a group of friends or your dog a couple of times a week;
- got your hair cut regularly so you felt good about the way you look; and
- scheduled and took a vacation that let you disconnect the way you want to.

You can. How do I know? For almost two decades, I've been on the front lines creating new, more modern and flexible ways of managing work and life. I've worked with tens of thousands of individuals and hundreds of organizations, including JPMorgan Chase, JCPenney, Ernst & Young, the U.S. Navy, and the United Nations.

I've given individuals the tools to create successful flexibility plans that change the way they work (through telecommuting or more flexible hours) in order to manage their lives off the job. And I've shown organizations how to use these same flexible work solutions to make their business more productive, save money, and provide better customer service.

Over those years, I've learned seven truths about work and life in our modern, hectic world. These truths challenge many of our long-standing, core beliefs. The first three emerged as I began to study work+life issues in the early 1990s and continued up to the publication of my first book, *Work+Life: Finding the Fit That's Right for You* (Riverhead), in 2004. But as I promoted that book, I became aware of an important piece missing from the work+life puzzle. This discovery led me to the last four truths and, ultimately, to the *Tweak It* practice you'll find in these pages.

Before we go any further, it's important to note that *Tweak It* doesn't let employers and the government off the hook. Flexibility in the way work is done is critical if we—corporations, government, and individuals—are going to compete and succeed in today's highly competitive, 24/7 global economy.[1] Therefore, employers have to create work environments that truly support and encourage conversations about mutually beneficial, flexible work+life solutions.[2]

The government needs to update public policies that are woefully ill suited to modern times. This includes outdated tax policies that penalize out-of-state teleworkers, overtime regulations that make it difficult for hourly nonexempt workers to access flexibility in the way they work,[3] and a Social Security policy that penalizes working after you begin to draw benefits.[4]

And we, as individuals, need to learn how to reset the way work fits into life when we experience major life events like having a baby, caring for an aging adult, going back to school, or working in retirement. *But none of these broader changes will succeed unless they are supported by a foundation of everyday contentment and order that only we can build for ourselves.* This is why *Tweak It* is the important piece that's been missing from this big, complex puzzle. Until now. And it starts by acknowledging the seven modern truths about work and life.

Truth #1: There is a new work+life reality for all of us.

In the early 1990s, I was put in charge of the day-to-day management of a group of commercial bankers. At the time, there wasn't a need to train people how to fit work into the other parts of their lives. It was pretty clear. A workshop would have taken three minutes, including Q & A:

"When you walk in the door of the office at 9 a.m. Monday through Friday, that's when you begin work. After you walk out the door at 5 p.m., or when you're on your two guaranteed weeks of vacation when no one will be able to reach you, that's when you take care of everything else. If, for whatever reason, you can't walk in the door and work from nine to five in the office Monday through Friday, then we don't want you."

While it is true that not everyone in the early 1990s worked under these conditions, this was the standard set of rules that most people used to guide when they were supposed to work and when they were supposed to deal with the other responsibilities in their lives.

But I began to notice a subtle shift. The reality of people's lives no longer matched those neat, rigid expectations. The growing mismatch caused people and business to suffer, but at the time, it felt like I was the only person who thought this was a problem that needed solving.[5]

I was a newly minted first-time manager overseeing a group of commercial bankers and administrators. I was married but didn't have children, so I could work that Monday through Friday schedule for as many hours as I wanted. That wasn't the case for my staff and colleagues, many of whom had children.

One day my supervisor approached my desk and said, "You need to put Jack on probation." "What?" I responded with confusion. She continued, "Haven't you noticed he's coming in late, leaving early, taking long lunches, and talking on the phone most of the day, and he's not booking

INTRODUCTION   *xi*

any new business?" Naively, I pointed out, "Yes, but his wife just had a new baby, so I'm giving him some leeway." I was shocked by her response, which was something along the lines of "We have hours and goals." In other words, new fathers get no flexibility. As it turned out, neither did new mothers.

Around the same time, my colleague Linda had a baby. This was her first child in her recent second marriage. For more than a decade, she'd been a single mother who had successfully managed and grown some of the most high-profile accounts in the group. Before there was any formal announcement that Linda wasn't coming back from maternity leave, Linda's accounts were reassigned to me. Linda had chosen to quit, knowing how inflexible the office was about parenting demands. I knew there had to be a better way.

In fact there was, and it came to my attention from a somewhat surprising source—a sixty-year-old male CEO of a major bank, who was one of Linda's former clients. I had taken over his account and set up a meeting to introduce myself. After politely, but directly, pointing out his disappointment over Linda's departure, this distinguished CEO explained how he gave employees the flexibility to work from home or to change their hours. I'd never heard anything like this before. My head was spinning as I absorbed what he said. "Cali, you may think I'm flexible because I'm a nice guy. No, the reason I give my people some flexibility is because they stay with me forever. It's just good business."

This business leader was ahead of his time. He not only observed the same mismatch between rigid work expectations and life realities that I saw, but he was doing something about it. He had figured out that you closed the growing gap by creating new rules. Could companies really be more flexible in how, when, and where people did their jobs? Since it was the early 1990s, I was curious if anyone else was asking that question. I soon discovered that this CEO and I were not alone.

I became obsessed with learning as much as I could about new and innovative ways to address the transformation of work and life. Before I knew it, the folder of articles I'd gathered on the topic was six inches thick. Through my research, I learned that there was a small but growing group of academics, think tank experts, and business leaders who recognized the fundamental change in the expectations of what life on and off the job should look like. They understood that people and employers needed to update the traditional and increasingly obsolete Industrial Age guidelines that had been the rules of the road for decades. I wanted to be part of that effort. I decided to become a work+life strategy consultant.

I knew an MBA would help me convince corporate leaders that these issues were critical to the success of their business and their people. The credential would make it harder to dismiss my arguments with "That's nice, but you don't understand business." So, in 1993, I enrolled at Columbia Business School.

There were only two jobs in the whole country I wanted. Even though I knew no one in the small, emerging work+life field, I had faith something would work out. Updated, contemporary ways of managing work and life would become a strategic imperative. Momentous changes in demographics, technology, and the global economy were happening too rapidly to make it possible to stay stuck in an obsolete, rigid work/life model.

By the early to mid-1990s, America Online had introduced the first commercial e-mail system, which marked the start of what became the 24/7 work reality. However, working from home, flexible hours, reduced schedules, job sharing, or compressed workweeks still hadn't gone mainstream. Undeterred, I forged ahead with my plans.

Truth #2: We can and must be our own advocate.

In 1995, through a combination of luck, faith, and hard work, I landed my dream job as a work+life strategy consultant at the Families and Work Institute, the leading New York–based research think tank on issues related to work, life, and family. I was working with Dana Friedman, Ellen Galinsky, and Arlene Johnson, three of the most innovative trailblazers in the work+life field. Now, I was learning directly from the people who had inspired me from a distance for more than five years.

The expectations were high and the learning curve intense. So intense that when Arlene Johnson retired a few years ago, I wrote about the experience in my tribute to her, "It was like I decided to learn to play tennis and my first game was with world champions at Wimbledon." I had to figure out a lot, fast.

Almost immediately I realized that *companies and managers alone couldn't solve the work+life challenges of their employees.* This directly contradicted one of the core beliefs I held going into the field. Like most people then and many people today, I thought that if we just helped human resources departments create the right flexible-work-arrangement policies and communicated them well, if we opened the best child care centers, and if we developed the best training programs for managers, all of the problems would be solved.[6] Yet my work in a number of organizations proved to me that these efforts were only half of the equation.

Managers and HR departments can't tell each person in the organization how to manage their work and life, because everyone's circumstances on and off the job are completely different. People have to partner with their employers.

Employers must create a work environment in which it is okay to discuss potential flexible work+life solutions.[7] Then we individual employees need to meet the organization halfway and come to the table with a plan that takes into consideration our needs and the needs of the business. The problem was then and is now that most people had no idea what that meant or how to do it. How do you create a plan that made sense for you and your job? How do you discuss it with your boss and your team? And then once you got the okay, how do you make that flexibility succeed day to day?

It was 1997, and I searched high and low for the how-to guidelines that laid out the steps. When I discovered they didn't exist, I decided to develop the process based on my unique experience on the front lines in companies. First step: get rid of the term *work/life balance.*

Truth #3: The goal is work+life "fit," not "balance."

It was clear to me that the using *balance* to describe the goal of flexibility for individuals caused more problems than it solved.[8] For example, every time I met with a senior leader in an organization, I'd explain why it was a strategic imperative to give employees flexibility to manage their work/life balance. But before I could finish the first sentence, it was as if someone flipped off a light switch. You could see the executive shut down and stop listening.

I'd work with individuals to help them try to find their own balance and they'd have a similarly unproductive response. The conversation would end with a statement like "I don't have balance" and never moved to solutions. That's because there really isn't a balance, or ideal 50-50 split, between work and life. The word *balance* itself was a roadblock. In order for there to be any progress it needed to be removed. But how do you get past the concept when it's so deeply embedded in our culture as *the* most vital goal?

One day as I was interviewing yet another senior leader about his organization's flexibility strategy, I launched into my usual explanation about the imperative to give employees the flexibility to manage their work/life balance. As if on cue, his eyes began to glaze over. I'd lost him completely. I tried to reengage by talking about how frustrating it was to lose a valuable employee and how much his business would benefit from the extra productivity employees give when they have work/life balance.

Seeing me struggle, he decided to come clean, "Look, Cali, I appreciate what you're saying. But every time you say 'work/life balance,' all I hear is 'work less,' and we have so much work to do, I need everyone to do more. Plus I don't have any kind of work/life balance myself. How can I support something I don't have?"

Suddenly, I found myself saying, "But it's not about working less for most people, most of the time. It's about working differently. Shifting your hours, working from home, changing the way the work is done so that everyone can manage the way work fits into his or her life given their unique circumstances. The goal is to create an environment where all of those different work+life fit realities can live together to achieve the goals of business over time. You may not have work/life balance, but you do have a work+life fit."

Suddenly, his eyes lit up. It was as if someone had flipped the light switch back on. He said enthusiastically, "I get it. Yes, even though I do work a lot, I try to play tennis twice a week and I make sure I get to most of my son's soccer games. But I also realize that not everyone who works for me can do the same thing." By shifting the conversation from "balance" to "fit," I'd found the magic key that unlocked the door I'd kept banging up against for three years. One little word, *fit*, changed the conversation from resistance to possibility.[9]

As I began to use the work+life fit language, others had the same "aha" response. Because of the universally positive reaction, I assumed everyone would immediately embrace "fit." I underestimated the remarkable resilience of "balance."

Truth #4: Major life events matter, but it's the everyday routine we crave.

In the late 1990s, advances in technology began to accelerate. Mobile phones shrank and became more affordable. Soon everyone felt they needed to be immediately accessible day or night. Dial-up Internet service meant you could read e-mails and work from home. And business began to move into new and emerging global markets, expanding traditional hours of operations beyond local time zones. The few remaining physical boundaries that existed between life on and off the job were now gone.[10] The rigid guidelines that told us when we were supposed to work and get everything else done in our lives were officially irrelevant.

Not surprisingly, as I predicted, discussions about flexibility in the workplace became more commonplace and were less likely to be met with a confused "What?" Working from home, flexible hours, reduced schedules, job sharing, and compressed workweeks were increasingly recognizable concepts. These new, more flexible ways of fitting work into life weren't broadly available, but at least they weren't dismissed outright. Progress was happening, but more needed to be done.

In retrospect, what was interesting about this period was how the work+life field (myself included) focused exclusively on new ways to manage work and life in response to major life events. If you had a baby, could you work from home every Wednesday? If your father got sick, could you work ten hours four days a week and take every Monday off to care for him? If you went back to school, could you change your hours to come in earlier and leave earlier in order to get to class on time?

I thought I'd given people what they wanted and needed the most when my first book, *Work+Life: Finding the Fit That's Right for You*, was published. It was the simple, step-by-step guide for anyone who'd experienced a major moment of change.[11] It explained how to create, negotiate, and implement a plan that formally changed how, when, or where you worked for an extended period of time. I'd focused on the big transitions and resets because I assumed everyone had the small, everyday management of their work and life under control. I was wrong.

As I traveled the country promoting my first book, I kept hearing the same thing over and over: "I'd love to change my hours, work from home, or reduce my schedule, but I can't even get a date / get to the gym / see my friends (assuming I still have friends) / tuck my kid in one night a week / get a physical / pay my bills / get to the dry cleaner before it closes / buy a birthday present."

At first, I didn't pay much attention. Then, after hearing a similar story repeated enough times, I began to listen more closely. People were searching for a sense of day-to-day well-being and order on and off the job, a sense that was obviously missing. Nothing had replaced the old, obsolete 1960s guidelines that that told us clearly when it was "work" time and when it was "me" time. They wanted to know what the new rules were, and so did I. They hungered to move past the uncertainty and stress and find a way to love their jobs and lives again. But where to begin?

Truth #5: We may think we manage our work and life, but most of us don't.

I decided to start by unlocking the secrets of the people whom I call the work+life fit "naturals." These are individuals who intuitively and naturally seem to know how to make what matters to them happen when everyone else around them flounders. They innately know how to fit all of the pieces together, often without breaking a sweat.

I'd categorize about 10 to 15 percent of the population as work+life fit naturals. You can identify them two ways:

• Their coworkers point them out by saying something like "You should talk to Diane. She always seems to have this work+life fit thing all figured out. She's got three kids, her husband works, she's training for a marathon, and she's always happy. Seriously, I'm not sure she's human."

• Naturals will often approach me either before or after an event and say, "I'm sorry, please don't be offended, but why are you here? Isn't this information all pretty straightforward? Doesn't everyone do it?" For them, it's as if someone held a meeting to explain how you get out of bed in the morning and brush your teeth. They are genuinely perplexed as to why people need a step-by-step explanation about something that seems so obvious.

For naturals, managing their lives on and off the job is in their DNA. And they have a lot to teach the rest of us.

One of my most memorable encounters with a work+life fit natural almost ended in disaster. A couple of years ago I spoke to a group of six hundred junior-level accountants at one of the Big Four professional services firms. The senior managing partner who was going to introduce me came up at the cocktail party before the speech, shook my hand, and said, "It's so nice to meet you, but I don't understand why you are here." (My radar went off immediately.)

He began to explain how he was a rabid Penn State football fan, and when he was a junior-level accountant he made it clear that during football season, "I go to all of the weekend games. I would talk to the scheduler on Monday morning and explain how I needed to be off on Saturday. He or she would then give me extra work during the week, especially in busy season, so I could be at the game. It worked out fine. I don't understand why this is so hard."

I gently pointed out to him, "Well, you are what I call a work+life fit natural. Making small, ongoing tweaks in your work and life seems obvious to you. I can guarantee that most of these six hundred junior accountants in the room tonight don't have any idea how to do it." I could tell he thought I was nuts. He politely shook my hand and walked away. Needless to say, I couldn't wait to hear his introduction.

We filed into the auditorium, and the senior managing partner bounded onto the stage. He began, "To be honest, I didn't have any idea why we hired our speaker to present to you tonight. It's always been pretty clear to me how to flexibly manage the things you have to do at work with what you want to do in your life outside of work. And I guess until tonight I just assumed everyone else did, too. But I spent some time talking with many of you earlier, and you don't have a clue! So, thank goodness she's here to set you straight. And with that, let me introduce Cali Williams Yost..."

In my search to unlock their secrets, I'd ask any work+life fit natural I met how they did it. Over time, I began to see a pattern. There were a few simple steps most of the naturals followed without being conscious of it. These steps became the *Tweak It* practice you will be introduced to in chapter 3.

Once I understood the steps that were intuitive to the naturals, I realized they were almost completely missing from the routines of everyone else. Yet, when I'd point this out, I'd get a surprising amount of denial and pushback in return: "But, Cali, I swear I'm already actively managing my everyday work+life fit, and it's still not working." After I heard this enough times, I realized that most of us genuinely *believe* that we actively manage our everyday work+life fit, even if we don't. Perception doesn't match reality. But how do you motivate people to learn a new practice that will give them what they crave when they think that they're already doing it?

I decided that I needed proof. I started to ask people scheduled to attend one of my presentations to complete a brief presession survey. In total, 242 full-time working adults who attended eight different presentations answered the questions. Across industries and groups, their responses were basically the same. You will hear more about the results of this survey in chapter 4, but here's a summary:

• A majority of the respondents genuinely believe that they actively manage their everyday work and life on a regular basis. Seventy-five percent agreed that "on average, I actively manage my work and personal responsibilities and goals *daily or weekly.*"

But as they answered the next questions, the gap between perception and the reality began to show:

• Only 40 percent agreed that "I *always* keep a calendar with all of my personal and work to-dos and goals in one place." Most didn't have a clear snapshot of their work and personal activities and priorities in one place, which is critical for making good decisions.

• Twenty-six percent agreed that "On average, I set time aside *daily or weekly* to check in with myself and answer the question, 'What do I want?'" In other words, less than a third regularly reflected on what mattered to them. You can't take action without knowing what you want. And finally…

• Only 15 percent said, "When I see a mismatch between what I want in my work+life fit and what's happening I make adjustments, *always.*" Only 15 percent, or very few, said they took control and added what was missing and stopped what wasn't working. Interestingly, this percentage matches my estimate of the number of work+life fit naturals in the population.

No wonder most of us often feel like corks bobbing on a sea of everyday chaos. In all fairness, no one trains us to manage our work and our lives. And many of us keep waiting for someone else—someone outside or above us—to tell us what to do. According to our most recent national study of full-time employees in the United States, the 2011 Work+Life Fit Reality Check, 73 percent of respondents said they still believe that "work/ life flexibility is only possible if my employer and/or boss provides it."[12] That's an example of obsolete thinking in action. You can't wait. My purpose in this book is to teach you how to take control and make what matters to you happen, personally and professionally. Because, if not you, then who? Honestly, the answer is no one.

I'd decoded the secrets of the work+life fit naturals, and the *Tweak It* practice was born. Now I had to test it. The response was more than I could have imagined.

Truth #6: Small, regular actions make a big impact.

Proof is everywhere that small changes pay off over time. You lose two sizes by tracking your daily calories with Weight Watchers. You fund a European vacation by automatically transferring fifty dollars a week to savings. It's the same with managing the way work fits into your life day to day. *Tweak It* harnesses the small, targeted actions related to wellness, your job skills, networking, social media, finances, relationships, and personal maintenance for an equally powerful return. Soon enough, these barely noticeable choices will become second nature and collectively transform your performance both on the job and off without any scary, bold disruption. There's no one-size-fits-all balance, which you'll never achieve. It's about powering success at work and at home every day in subtle, practical ways.

As I developed the *Tweak It* practice, I reviewed other popular personal productivity tools. I was struck by how complicated many of them were. They got points for being comprehensive and covering every possible base, but I couldn't understand how someone with the demands of a real life and a real job was supposed to make them part of an already overloaded weekly routine. If *Tweak It* were going to become part of an already busy life, it would have to be simple and straightforward.

Before I introduced the *Tweak It* practice to my clients, I tested it myself. In addition to running my business, I'm also a wife, a mother of two, a daughter, a sister, and a friend. Honestly, at first, I was skeptical that a practice of small, deliberate choices would create order out of my work+life chaos. But it did, and it still does.

Finally, in 2006, after months of testing, I was ready to introduce the practice to my clients. I thought people would like it, but I had no idea how much they'd love it! The enthusiastic response confirmed how desperate people were. I watched in awe as the spark of hope and possibility caught fire in front of my eyes.

Not only did they like the simplicity and concreteness of the *Tweak It* practice, but they had fun! As people shared their tweaks and brainstormed with each other about the small changes that would have the biggest impact on their work+life fit, you could see smiles on everyone's face and hear laughter throughout the room. In less than ninety minutes, the atmosphere shifted from frustration to a sense of possibility and optimism. Here's some of the feedback I received after teaching the *Tweak It* practice:

> The group was unbelievably engaged, asked many questions and stayed to talk to Cali after the presentation. Every single one of the attendees filled out an evaluation form—which is unusual—and all had glowing comments concerning how relevant and motivating it was.
>
> The bottom line is that work-life fit is always something that people want to learn more about and really want to solve. I think today people are extremely busy and stressed about work. It was clearly highly relevant and motivating to everyone who attended. It was very, very well received.
>
> Cali suggested very specific actions to address work-life fit, which I thought was the most motivating part of her presentation. She had real, everyday examples—the small things you can do to build fit into your life. It was immediately actionable and relevant.
>
> —*Fortune 500* consumer products company

Work-life fit is such a foreign concept to a military organization, especially to our "middle management"—commanders and captains who can find it difficult to implement within the fleet. Work+Life Fit helped us strategize ways to engage personnel at that level so they have a better understanding of how small changes could have a big impact on the individual level. One senior participant was getting ready to take command of a ship, and she stood up during Cali's presentation and said, "I really had an aha moment," realizing that small changes could have a significant impact on people's lives.

Military personnel don't have a tremendous amount of control over their own work-life balance. Cali excelled at getting people to look at it from an individual level, and finding ways to present it as a partnership to their leaders. That's what resonated with our audience; they were given the tools to improve their own quality of life while still working within the chain of command.

—U.S. Navy

What I learned from watching these groups and many others over the years is that the real power of *Tweak It* is unleashed when we do it together. Whether it's sharing the small activities and priorities that made the most difference to us or supporting someone else so they can make a meaningful tweak happen, you begin to see that we, collectively, can build a foundation of contentment, well-being, and order that goes beyond our own everyday work+life fit.

Truth #7: Together we can start the Tweak It *revolution.*

About the same time I began to research and develop the *Tweak It* practice, I discovered the power of virtual communities (for example, blogs and social media) to bring like-minded people together. For the first time,

I wasn't the lone voice in the wilderness shouting "We have to transform the way we manage our work and life" and wondering if anyone else heard and agreed.

For years, I'd been frustrated with the coverage of work+life issues in the media. The reports didn't reflect what I saw on the front lines inside actual organizations when I was working with real people.

In 2005, the challenges facing upper-income working mothers dominated the news. Stories on the "opting out" revolution, off ramps and on ramps, and the mommy wars were everywhere.[13] While these issues were important and shined a spotlight on the desperate need for reliable, affordable child care and paid leave for all parents, they were a symptom of the broader problem that remained largely untouched by the media. Unfortunately, the symptom, not the problem, became *the* only story.

The problem, or the real story, was the radical mismatch between people's lives on and off the job and the outdated, inflexible expectations that still ruled the cultures of most organizations. Fortunately (or unfortunately), upper-income mothers could afford to respond with their feet and say, "Forget it. I'm out of here." This left everyone else who couldn't quit—the majority of mothers and fathers, elder-care providers, single people—stuck, and ignored by the media.

I decided to test what was then a new technology in an effort to refocus the debate back onto the sweeping transformation of work and life that was underway but had gone largely unnoticed. So I started blogging.

In January 2006, I launched my Work+Life Fit blog.[14] At first, the only regular readers were my husband, my mom (who used to leave public comments like "Great point, honey," not understanding everyone could see them) and my best friend. But slowly, it grew. And I began to meet other people online who shared their experiences, expertise, and opinions.

Then, in 2007, I was asked to blog for *Fast Company*,[15] and in 2010 I began to blog for *Forbes*.[16] (The hard work was rewarded when Forbes. com named the Work+Life Fit blog as one of the Top 100 Websites for

Women in 2010 and 2011.[17]) This connected me to a whole other universe of people who were grappling with what it means to work, live, and run a business in this new emerging world with no clear boundaries. Finally, I dove into Twitter, LinkedIn, and Facebook, and further expanded my community of knowledge, support, and change around this critical issue. I realized that this was a multifaceted, multinational, enormous community interested in shaping what the future of work and life looked like.

Now, with *Tweak It*, how could I harness the power of this wonderful virtual community to spread the excitement and fun I saw in the groups that had experienced the *Tweak It* practice live? Then one lovely summer evening I attended a U2 concert with my husband and the picture became clear.

I watched as Bono stepped onto the stage and sang the first few lines of the song "I Still Haven't Found What I'm Looking For." Then he stopped, and held the microphone out to the crowd. Suddenly, fifty thousand people in Giants Stadium took over and began to sing. Bono danced around the stage, joyfully listening as we, the crowd, finished what he'd started with our unique, imperfect voices singing in unison. At that moment, I understood how the power of a shared experience could start a *Tweak It* revolution. Here's how we'll do it together:

Each week, I'll share my Tweaks of the Week (chapter 5) in the *Tweak It* online community (www.tweakittogether.com) and then I want to hear from you. What are the small activities and priorities that you are going to make happen over the next seven days? Share it in a tweet on Twitter, a post on Facebook, or a video clip on YouTube. In addition to exchanging tips, inspirations, and insights with each other, experts from over fifty work, life, and career specialties will join us in the revolution. These wise and wonderful individuals share their simplest, get-started advice in the book (chapters 11–17) and in the *Tweak It* online community, so there's no excuse for not taking action because you don't know how to begin. The areas covered by their wisdom include the following:

Renew Tweaks
- ✓ Move Your Body
- ✓ Choose Healthy Food
- ✓ Prepare Healthy Meals
- ✓ Get More Sleep
- ✓ Learn to Meditate
- ✓ Do Nothing . . . Often
- ✓ Take a Vacation
- ✓ Celebrate Good Times
- ✓ Create, Dream, Escape
- ✓ Practice Your Faith
- ✓ Give Something Back
- ✓ Manage Tech Distraction

Career Tweaks
- ✓ Build Your Network
- ✓ Create Virtual You
- ✓ Update Your Skills
- ✓ Learn New Technologies
- ✓ Know Your Type
- ✓ For Younger Workers
- ✓ For Older Workers
- ✓ Plan a Career Break
- ✓ Find an Encore (Preretirement) Career
- ✓ Start Your Own Business

Money Tweaks
- ✓ Everyday Finances
- ✓ Retirement Savings
- ✓ College Savings

Connect Tweaks
- ✓ Loved Ones
- ✓ Friends
- ✓ Date
- ✓ Community

Connect with Kids Tweaks
- ✓ Kids under Thirteen Years
- ✓ Teens
- ✓ Just for Dads
- ✓ Nieces/Nephews
- ✓ Technology
- ✓ School
- ✓ College Planning
- ✓ SAT Prep

Caregiving Tweaks
- ✓ Elder Care—General
- ✓ Elder Care—with Siblings
- ✓ Child Care—Regular and Backup
- ✓ Summer Care

Maintenance Tweaks
- ✓ Your Health
- ✓ Your Personal Appearance
- ✓ Your Car
- ✓ Your House—Get Organized
- ✓ Your House—Clean It Yourself
- ✓ Your House—Hire Cleaning Help
- ✓ Your House—Maintain It

You deserve a life where what matters to you happens; where your personal and professional priorities fit together to create a foundation of everyday contentment, well-being, and order. But you must take the lead. And you start by acknowledging the seven modern truths about work and life:

- Truth #1: There is a new work+life reality for all of us.
- Truth #2: We can and must be our own advocate.
- Truth #3: The goal is work+life "fit," not "balance."
- Truth #4: Major life events matter, but it's the everyday routine we crave.
- Truth #5: We may *think* we manage our work and life, but most of us don't.
- Truth #6: Small, regular actions make a big impact.
- Truth #7: Together we can start the *Tweak It* revolution.

Then, make the simple *Tweak It* practice part of your weekly routine. You'll do this by:

- understanding who will benefit from *Tweak It* in chapter 1 (Hint: anyone who wants to love his or her life on and off the job in a complex, ever-changing world);
- recognizing the small price you must pay to enjoy the big payoffs of *Tweak It* in chapter 2;
- getting an overview of the *Tweak It* practice and then diving deeper into the three phases in chapters 3 to 6;
- learning in chapters 7 to 10 how Lisa, Jeff, Denise, and Pete, four people with very different personal and professional realities and goals, used the *Tweak It* practice to improve their lives one small step at a time; and
- finding simple, get-started advice from the fifty-plus *Tweak It* Inspiration experts in chapters 11 to 17.

Yes, fifteen years ago someone may have forgotten to send the memo with the new rules for finding time every day for what matters to you in a modern, hectic world. Now there's *Tweak It*. Let's get started.

How do you *Tweak It*?

Walk and Work

I do what's called work-walking on my treadmill. I bought a SurfShelf that hooks onto the treadmill. I walk at two miles an hour, which is just fast enough where you kind of burn calories and you still have the dexterity to use your mouse and keyboard. I create a to-do list for my treadmill time, such as watching a video someone sent me and answering e-mails.

—Lorie Marrero, author of *The Clutter Diet: The Skinny on Organizing Your Home and Taking Control of Your Life*

Bike to Work

I was challenged to the NYC triathlon by a former patient. At the time of the challenge, I was working eighty hours a week, eating fast food (or whatever was available in the cafeteria), and exercise was not a part of my life. I was approximately two hundred pounds. I bought a bicycle and began riding to work each day. Once the pounds started to come off, I found that I enjoyed how I looked and felt much more than I enjoyed food and wine. I eat when I'm hungry and stop when I'm full. I stay away from the fast food restaurants, never drink soda, and try to control stress. I do still enjoy a glass of scotch and the occasional cigar, so I'm by no means a true healthy-eating zealot!

—Allan Stewart, MD, director of the Aortic Surgery Program at NewYork-Presbyterian Hospital/Columbia University Medical Center

Chapter 1

Who Needs Tweak It?

Meet Charlie, Ellen, Carter, and Samantha

Charlie has been a technician for the same telecommunications company for fifteen years. He's the father of two boys, whom he loves to coach in football. His free time is spent either helping his aging father, who lives in the next town, or renovating his house with a friend. After a recent strike, he's beginning to think he may need a backup plan for his job. It does help that his wife is a nurse, even if it means he needs to do his share of cooking, laundry, and general day-to-day family maintenance. He looks forward to his annual fishing trip with his friends, and he tries to take care of himself physically because he knows it's the only way he'll be able to keep doing his job another twenty years, "knock on wood."

Ellen graduated from college two years ago and is a junior accountant at a large firm. In spite of almost nonstop travel to client offices, she's continuing her education with online courses. She's close to her large, extended family and is passionate about ballroom dancing. Personally, her short-term goal is to manage her money carefully so that she can move out of her parents' house. Professionally, she'd like to find a position in the finance department of an alternative energy company and is making a point to connect with groups and professionals in that industry. She recently met someone whom she really likes, but they struggle to find time to be together as much as they'd like.

Carter is a semiretired investment manager who would like to transition the remaining ownership of his firm to his partner within the next two years. A grandfather of four who's been married to his college sweetheart for forty-five years, he's also a part-time tree farmer and loves to travel and read. But that's not stopping him from wanting to find another part-time job that would allow him to give back to the community while bringing in some extra income. He's been exploring his options.

Samantha is a single parent of one son. She's worked in the customer-service department of a company for the last five years. Her commute is an hour each way, which doesn't leave much time at the end of the day to cook, do the laundry, maintain her car and town house, and see her son. She'd love to date, but doesn't know where to begin. Her wide circle of friends has been an invaluable source of support, and she's considering taking up yoga to manage her stress—but when?

Like Charlie, Ellen, Carter, and Samantha, most of us want and need to keep a job that pays the bills, especially today. We have lives that include family, friends, and interests outside of work that matter deeply to us. We have to maintain the place where we live and the car that we drive. We need to manage our money, plan for caregiving responsibilities, and think about how we are going to live in our later years. We require sleep, exercise, and healthy food to feel our best. And almost all of us are connected (often too connected) across all parts of our lives by technology.

These are the everyday activities and priorities that real people with real jobs and real lives struggle to control and master in a world where the rules of engagement have not been clear for a long time. In other words, most of us need to *Tweak It*.

But maybe "real people with real jobs and real lives" is too broad a description, and you're still not sure it includes you. So let's break it down further. Like you, Charlie, Ellen, Carter, and Samantha are members of at least one of the six specific groups of people who, for different reasons, will benefit from a weekly practice of powerful small actions made deliberately and consistently. They include women, men, Gen-Y/Millennials, adult caregivers, "retirees" who work, and entrepreneurs.

Women (partnered, single, mothers, and nonmothers)

Tweak It is for women *and* men; however, it's important to emphasize that women are the ones who have tried their best to bring the growing work and life mismatch to the world's attention for the past two decades. The old strict rules of when you work and when you manage your life no longer align with the rapidly changing realities of everyone's responsibilities on and off the job. But because women bear children and often are the primary parent (although increasingly less so[1]), the perception became that this mismatch was a "women's issue."[2] The historic transformation of work and life was the real problem, but the most noticeable symptom, pregnancy and child care, became the focus.

We are aware of a colleague's pregnancy, but we can't easily see a coworker care for a sick parent or a handicapped adult sibling, take an evening class, have a phone conference at night with a client in another time zone, or manage a chronic illness.

When a baby is born, a mother is not at work for a period of time, which again is noticeable. After the new mother returns to work (assuming she returns), she now has a different set of circumstances on and off the job, which can be noticeable as well. When we connect the visible pregnancy with the noticeable absence and the assumed change in circumstances, it's easy to conclude that the conflict between lives at work and at home must be about women having children. Even when the research consistently proves that it's not.[3]

When I point out the inaccuracy of this perception, people will push back and say, "Yes, but men who have children and people with aging parents don't disappear from work for three to six months like mothers do." Actually, in both instances the disappearance can occur faster and be more acute. Elder care or illness often happens suddenly and unexpectedly, whereas most of the time people have months to plan for the absence of a pregnant coworker. And, usually, the date the mother is expected to return is predetermined and easy to plan around as well. I've witnessed countless cases over the years where, without notice, people are out of work for weeks or months because of a heart attack or the severe illness of a parent. And while men may not disappear for months after a baby is born, new fathers also experience a meaningful shift in priorities that requires them to change their everyday work+life fit.[4] But that shift is not as visual. We don't *see* that a new father was pregnant, so we don't make the direct link to the change.

While efforts to support working mothers have been helpful and well intentioned, they've also inadvertently reinforced the already pervasive "mommy penalty"[5] that unfairly targets and limits women's career advancement. This is the misperception that women, particularly mothers, are the only group that struggles with their responsibilities on and off the job and are, therefore, unemployable. The truth is that men are reporting higher levels of conflict between their work and personal lives than women, but again there aren't the same visual clues, so we miss it.

I hope that *Tweak It* finally broadens the focus beyond motherhood and places it back on addressing how the historic, radical transformation in work and life over the past two decades has affected all of us.

Men (partnered, single, fathers, and nonfathers)

If you are a man, then reading *Tweak It* may be first time that you've:

- picked up a book or participated in a community about how to better manage your day-to-day work+life fit;

- felt like you were a welcomed and valued participant in that conversation; and
- realized that you are not the only guy who wants to make what matters to him happen as part of a successful career.

Coincidentally, as I started writing this chapter, my aunt told me the following story. It's about her recent experience recruiting a new dean for the community college at which she is a long-time professor. Her story illustrates perfectly how senior-level men are beginning to seek and prioritize the ability to work and have a life. She wrote:

I was on a hiring committee for our new dean. It took a year for us to find the right person, and did we get a winner! I was also part of the group that wrote the position announcement and job description. The job description really was looking for a Super Man or Woman. It was an impossible description for any one person to fill. We discussed burnout and were concerned we would use up the successful candidate, if we could find him/her. But—we found him—and at our first kickoff meeting of the academic year, I gave him a Superman coffee mug. He keeps it prominently displayed in his workspace as a testament to our support for him.

He has two young children, and many days he leaves work mid-to-late afternoon to pick up the children from school. Other days he is there until 6 or 7 or even 8, and he responds to e-mails sometimes well into the night. I believe he also coaches one of the children's sports teams. In one of our conversations, he reminded me that the job description had a bullet item about work+life fit— that the successful candidate would be able to manage that. He said that impressed him about this position.

Men want and need the flexibility to make what matters to them happen just as much as women do.[6] But historically they've been excluded overtly and subtly from the work+life issue. I've witnessed several examples of this over the years:

- In many organizations, the responsibility for addressing work+life issues is part of the Women's Initiative.
- HR leaders would hire me to work with their employees and dismiss my prediction that men would participate if they were invited by saying, "Don't be disappointed if they don't show up." They were invariably shocked when almost half of the audience was men.
- In most mainstream media outlets, work+life challenges and solutions are discussed in the style sections of newspapers, on morning talk shows aimed at women, or in women's magazines.

No wonder men haven't felt welcomed or included. The message has been that the discussion about how to fit your work and personal life together doesn't apply to you. And, if you're having trouble, you're the only one who is: "Dude, there must be something wrong with you."

Not only are men reporting higher levels of work+life conflict than women are,[7] but a clear majority of adults surveyed who work full-time believe work/life balance is an issue for everyone, not just women.[8] Therefore, it wasn't surprising that another round of recent studies all found that men face many if not more of the challenges managing their responsibilities on and off the job than women do.[9]

Men's benefits from the *Tweak It* practice include creating a strong professional network, updating their skills, strengthening their personal finances, managing the caregiving for their children and aging relatives, connecting with friends, and making time for sports and fitness.

Yes, I hope *Tweak It* finally puts to rest the myth that work+life fit is a women's issue, but I want men to know that the *Tweak It* practice and community are 100 percent meant for them as well. I hope men become active and enthusiastic participants in the *Tweak It* revolution. In fact, nothing will truly shift without men onboard. Some of my most powerful partners for change over the years inside of companies have been men. Their voices on this issue are valuable and important. I hope to hear many more!

Gen-Ys/Millennials

Gen-Ys/Millennials have gotten an incredibly bad rap in the workplace and in the media for their supposed obsession with work/life balance.[10] For these digital natives, technology connects all parts of their lives on and off the job all of the time. I often joke that if I could get the people under thirty years old who work for my corporate clients into a soundproof room they'd say, "Why do we have to come to the same place at the same time every day to get work done?" They don't understand the lingering, outdated rule that says work is nine to five in the office, Monday through Friday, and life outside of work happens after that.[11] Like working mothers, Millennials have been waving a red flag that points to a bigger issue, which is that we all need updated, more contemporary, and flexible ways to manage work and life.

Unfortunately, instead of listening, we've interpreted their arguments for balance as "I don't want to work hard." Yes, there will always be poor performers in every generation. But what I see, more often than not, is the willingness to work hard but also the desire to work differently and more flexibly. In other words, "I'll finish that report tonight at home, but it's a beautiful day and I want to leave early and go to the ball game." The work will get done on time. It just might get done at night.

I recently interviewed a younger employee who works for one of my corporate clients. When I asked her about older managers who still resist letting her work from home, she chuckled and said, "Give it five years, and when we're in charge it will just be normal." I agree, but in the meantime, there is one area where the *Tweak It* practice can help Gen-Y/Millennials more effectively harness their innate work+life flexibility so they can do what matters to them.

The consistent complaint I hear from managers about younger employees and their pursuit of balance is that they sometimes don't adequately consider the needs of the business or their colleagues. For example, a manager told me this story: "I have a young guy who works for me. He always gets his job done, but because he's still learning, he requires supervision. He often asks me if he can finish projects at home in the evening or over the weekend. In theory, I don't have a problem with that; however, in practice it's tough. The problem is that I'm the person he comes to when he needs a question answered, and I have a family. Therefore, I am not always near e-mail or my mobile phone when he has an issue to discuss. It just doesn't work for me."

If that Millennial employee had a way to think through the impact of working on the project from home in advance—how it would affect this boss, his team, and so on—chances are he'd receive a more positive reception for his request. That communication and coordination process is part of the *Tweak It* practice.

You'll pick the small activities and priorities you want to incorporate into your work+life fit for the week. Then, you'll consider whom you need to talk to at work and in your personal life in order to make that tweak succeed for everyone. For Millennials, this more thoughtful, organized approach could increase support from their managers for the kind of flexibility that's such a no-brainer to them but is unfortunately misunderstood by others.

Adult caregivers

I'm often asked, "Seriously, Cali, people have been trying to bring the way we live and work into the twenty-first century for more than two decades. What's going to be the tipping point that finally gets the attention of the powers that be?" My simple answer is "Elder care." Why? In one year, 65 million people will care for a chronically ill, disabled, or aged family member or friend twenty to forty hours a week on average.[12] Currently, a quarter of adult children will provide this type of care to a parent. These responsibilities exact a heavy toll on the caregiver, physically, emotionally, and financially.[13]

Millions of us will face the difficult and expensive task of having to work while caring for an aging adult, especially as the huge Baby Boomer population gets older.[14] This doesn't even include the millions of people who work while caring for a disabled child or an adult sibling.

I always had a professional understanding of the realities of elder care, but it wasn't until I supported my mother in the last few months of her life as she battled cancer that I truly appreciated just how uniquely difficult it can be.[15] Elder care makes child care look like a walk in the park for the following reasons:

• Whereas most children grow and mature at a predictable, consistent rate, each adult requiring care is different in terms of his or her needs and the progression of his or her illness.

• While child care is exhausting, at least you can see the effort as a positive investment toward the future. With elder care, it's exhausting and it supports the end of someone's life journey, and that takes an emotional toll.

• With children, you are the adult and have control. With other adults, they have veto power and don't have to comply.

Because it's simple and straightforward, *Tweak It* is particularly relevant for the needs of adult caregivers who are trying to fulfill their responsibilities outside of work and keep their jobs. It fills a void of work+life fit how-to information that leaves too many working caregivers stranded and overwhelmed. If you're part of the rapidly increasing ranks of elder-care givers . . . welcome!

"Retirees" who work

If you are part of the generation approaching retirement, then you can relate to the days when a training session on how to work and manage the other parts of your life would have taken three minutes including Q & A. You grew up with the inflexible "nine to five, in the office, Monday through Friday" rule of thumb that governed the way we worked and lived. And even though it's now obsolete, those guidelines are still part of your belief system. For most of your career, you didn't have to take control and actively manage your daily work and life so that what mattered to you happened. The boundaries between "work" time and "me" time were rigid and clear.

More Baby Boomers are directly challenging the part of that old rulebook that said by sixty-five years old, you are completely retired and not working.[16] A 2010 study of 9,100 employees by Towers Watson found that 40 percent of workers are planning to retire later than they were two years prior. Many are looking for new "encore" careers that allow them to earn money and work for a cause they feel passionate about,[17] while others plan to continue to work in their current jobs.[18] They're creating a new "working retirement." This is a real trend when you go to the AARP website and find a separate section entitled "Work & Retirement."[19]

If you are a working retiree, the *Tweak It* practice shows you how to take control over the way work fits into your life in this new phase. You can make sure that the activities and priorities that keep you healthy are part of your routine, along with the hobbies and experiences you don't want to put off until "retirement."

Entrepreneurs

When I present to a group of people inside of a company, I'm often asked, "So, Cali, what's your work+life fit?" I'm more than happy to share. I explain that "I'm a mother of two, a wife, and I work for myself primarily out of my home office unless I'm at a client site as I am today." Someone in the crowd will inevitably reply, "What do you know about work+life conflict. You have the perfect situation." I always respectfully respond, with a smile, "It may look perfect to you, but working for yourself isn't always the personal and professional nirvana you might imagine."

The truth is I'm an accidental entrepreneur. I never imagined that I would work for myself. I don't come from a family of entrepreneurs, but I made the decision to strike out on my own and start my consulting firm because I wanted to:

- develop and implement corporate work+life flexibility strategies in the way I felt it needed to be done to succeed;
- have the ability to write my first book; and
- have control over my schedule in order to also take care of my new daughter.

I did achieve all three goals, but I also learned a very hard lesson. As an entrepreneur, I had to be even more vigilant and rigorous about when, how, and where I worked and where I focused on the other important parts of my life. If I didn't, work would consume me. This is why I need the *Tweak It* practice as much as everyone else.

Many would-be entrepreneurs tell me, "I want to strike out on my own because I want a work+life fit that's better than the one I have now, working for someone else." That's certainly a valid motivation, but it will only be worth it if you find that fit you envisioned. Perhaps more than being a person who works for or with others, you really have to take charge and make consistent, deliberate choices that ensure what truly matters to you happens as often as possible. This makes *Tweak It* is an invaluable practice for every entrepreneur.

Who Needs Tweak It? *Summary:*

Who needs the *Tweak It* practice? Anyone who wants to love their lives on and off the job, especially women, men, Millennials, preretirees, and entrepreneurs. Chances are that includes you!

What's Next:

In chapter 2 we'll compare the small price you'll pay to be part of the *Tweak It* revolution with the three major payoffs you will realize.

How do you *Tweak It*?

Blog and Tweet Your Way to a Promotion

I recently met a man who was living in Atlanta but wanted to move back to his company's headquarters in Michigan. Even though there weren't too many people in finance who used Twitter to share information, he decided to start sharing links to articles related to finance and consumer goods. He also began to write a blog. It required more time but showcased his ideas about newsworthy topics that had to do with his field. Over time, he began to get known within his company. He would go to conferences and people would say, "I know you. You're . . . ," because they followed him on Twitter or had read his blog. It didn't take too long before he wound up getting the job he wanted back at headquarters.

—Miriam Salpeter, author of *Social Networking for Career Success*

Take a Tech-Free Sunday

Many Sundays are what I call a tech-free Sunday. Most of my good friends know this. They'll text me, but I don't open my computer. I do not read e-mail. I don't go to CNN.com. I might read the physical paper. I might have my phone on, but I'm not on Twitter. I'm not on Facebook. I've accepted that a majority of the time this means I'm working a longer Monday to catch up. I have to go in a little bit earlier and plan for the week ahead of time because I'm a boss and there's a lot that happens. But I won't do it on Sundays.

—Sloane Berrent, founder of www.thecausemopolitan.com

Chapter 2

Small Price and Big Payoffs of Tweak It

"Does this really work?" asked a participant in one of my recent workshops.

"Yes," I responded, "if you do it."

There are two reasons that people commit to a change: (1) the benefits are compelling enough to make you want to do things differently, and/ or (2) the pain is great enough that you're willing to do what it takes to resolve it. In other words, the payoffs you'll realize must exceed the price you have to pay. With the *Tweak It* practice, the payoffs that make what matters to you happen are three times greater than the one simple price, which is commitment.

The Price of Tweak It

You will be introduced to the work+life fit *Tweak It* practice in the next chapter. It is so simple and straightforward that you can easily master it, but practice is the price that you'll have to pay for success. Your challenge will be to make room for *Tweak It* in your weekly routine. This can feel daunting, especially if the reason you picked up this book is that you already feel overwhelmed. Adding another to-do may seem impossible.

Yes, it only works if you're committed to making the consistent and conscious choices it encourages and supports, but *consistent* doesn't mean "perfect and always." That's a key point we'll cover. It means "*most* of the time," and we all can do that. But you have to *want* to.

You have to want to nurture your relationships with friends, partners, children, and parents. You have to want to maintain your employability by networking, taking a class that updates your skills, and creating an online professional presence. You have to want to feel better physically and emotionally because you eat healthier meals, move your body, take vacations, and find time for a special talent you may have ignored.

It means sitting down every week and devoting approximately thirty minutes to answering the question "What do I want?" and then figuring out how to make those Tweaks of the Week happen. That's the price you will pay to realize the following three big payoffs.

The three big payoffs of Tweak It

PAYOFF #1: YOU'RE MORE LIKELY TO KEEP YOUR JOB AND LOVE YOUR LIFE IN A HIGHLY COMPETITIVE, RAPIDLY CHANGING GLOBAL ECONOMY.

Bill Gross, founder and co–chief investment officer of the highly regarded and influential investment management firm PIMCO, said in a *Washington Post* editorial that one of the greatest challenges facing the global economy was "2 billion new competitive workers from Asia and elsewhere [taking] jobs and paychecks from complacent and ill-trained 40-somethings in developed markets."[1]

No doubt there's more global competition for jobs, but I don't think people in the developed world are "complacent." I think they're unaware and unprepared. There's a difference. People find their employability at risk, in part, because they are unhealthy, their skills aren't up to date, or they haven't created and maintained a professional network, in person and online. This lack of awareness and preparedness doesn't have to be permanent. Nor does it require a big, overwhelming, all-at-once change. There are a number of tweaks in the key areas related to employability and wellness that are part of the *Tweak It* practice. Together, these small, very doable actions help everyone bring the best of themselves to the workplace in a rapidly changing, competitive global economy.

Bob and Rich have the same job, in the same industry. Both are married with children and both love to play the guitar as a hobby. Bob hasn't adapted, and his struggle has compromised both his health and long-term employability. Rich, on the other hand, figured things out a while ago and adopted the *Tweak It* practice as part of his routine. He's taken control and made sure that what matters most to him is happening on a regular basis. Let's compare:

Bob's Story—Floundering without a foundation

Bob works on average fifty hours a week in an office, but is often on his BlackBerry or computer at home. He hasn't spent one-on-one time with his wife or children in months. He can't remember the last time he exercised, and he usually grabs a hot dog on the corner for lunch at his desk. So it wasn't surprising when he popped into a walk-in clinic to get antibiotics for a nagging sinus infection and found out he's thirty pounds overweight and has high blood pressure. He was told to see his doctor, but he's been too busy. Maybe he'll go next month when things quiet down.

He's aware of a new software program that's under development. It supposedly does the work he currently provides for his clients. It's not perfected and clients haven't bought it yet, but he hasn't had time to learn about the product or figure out how his service is different or better. He hasn't attended a local business-networking event in years, and doesn't have a profile on LinkedIn: "Who has the time to maintain it? Maybe next month." He recently heard through his wife that her friend's husband is starting a monthly jam session in his basement. While he's intrigued, he hasn't picked up his guitar in years. Maybe he'll get around to it next year. Right now, he's just too tired and overwhelmed.

Rich's Story—Tweak It *in action*

Rich works on average fifty hours a week mostly in an office but sometimes at home. It depends on what's happening at work on a particular day. In a given week, he tries to get up an hour earlier three days to exercise, even if it's just to walk the dog. On Sundays, he helps his wife grocery-shop and make a couple of simple, healthy meals for dinner that they can just pull out of the freezer and reheat. At least two nights a week, he tries to leave work by 6 p.m. and turns off his BlackBerry when he gets in the door. He leaves instructions that if people really need him they can call his home number. No one ever does, and he gets focused time with his family.

Periodically, in the evening, he and his wife make a commitment to quickly review their online budget account just to make sure they are on track with their spending and debt. At least once every three months, he blocks off a Saturday afternoon to update his LinkedIn profile, contribute a brief post to his industry association's blog, and schedule a local business-networking event on his calendar. At the last event, he participated in a class about a new software program that is supposed to be able to do the work he currently provides for his clients. He was able to see that the hype didn't match reality, and he prepared a letter for his clients explaining the program, what it does and doesn't do, and how his service adds value. They appreciated the update and even offered to give him more business.

And, he still finds room about once a month on Thursday night to meet with three other people in his friend's basement for a jam session. Playing his beloved guitar always makes him feel more creative and energized.

He makes these small, meaningful activities and priorities happen on a regular basis because he plans them. Here are Rich's tweaks in a typical week:

Monday	Tuesday	Wednesday	Thursday	Friday	Saturday	Sunday
Work 8:00 a.m. to 6:00 p.m. in office/turn off mobile phone	Work 8:30 a.m. to 6:30 p.m. in office	Work 8:30 a.m. to 6:30 p.m. in office	Work 8:00 a.m. to 6:00 p.m. from home/turn off mobile phone	Work 8:30 a.m. to 6:30 p.m. in office		
	Wake up at 7:00 a.m. to exercise	Wake up at 7:00 a.m. to exercise		Wake up at 7:00 a.m to exercise		
12:00 p.m.: Attend local networking group lunch					12:00 p.m. to 2:00 p.m.: Grocery-shop, prep meals for week with wife 2:00 p.m. to 3:00 p.m.: Update LinkedIn profile	Catch up on e-mail, plan for workweek two hours during day
6:30 p.m.: Dinner with family		8:00 p.m.: Review online budget with wife	6:30 p.m.: Dinner with family 7:30 p.m. to 9:30 p.m.: Jam session with friends			

Who's better prepared to bring the best of himself to the challenges of work in a competitive global economy? Bob or Rich? Rich, obviously, but if we're honest, we know a lot more people who look and act like Bob. Rich has created his own solid baseline of relationships, health, organization, and job viability in an uncertain economic era. And he does it one deliberate, conscious, and consistent choice at a time each day.

PAYOFF #2: YOU'LL HARNESS THE POWER OF SMALL, MANAGEABLE ACTIVITIES AND PRIORITIES THAT BUILD A FOUNDATION OF WELL-BEING AND ORDER.

The focus on small and manageable choices is especially important in a period of economic insecurity. Many people are hesitant to do anything too radical that would put their jobs in jeopardy.[2]

Recent academic research proves the power of small steps to create well-being and order in our everyday work+life fit. A study published by professors Glen E. Kriener, Elaine C. Hollensbe, and Mathew L. Sheep in the *Academy of Management Journal* (2009) talks about a concept called "boundary theory," or the way "people create, maintain, or change boundaries in order to simplify and classify the world around them."[3] They focused on how sixty Episcopal priests manage the inevitable conflicts that arise between their work and life in a job that can be 24/7, be unpredictable, and carry unrelenting responsibility.

Their findings confirm what I've discovered over the five years that I've worked with the *Tweak It* practice. The priests who maintained a sense of satisfaction and structure "enacted a variety of boundary work tactics." In other words, through a series of small, deliberate, ongoing actions, they created a positive day-to-day fit between their work and the other parts of their lives that met their needs and the demands of their job. For example, one priest took his cell phone on vacation in order to be accessible to his parishioners, but he had his wife answer and screen calls. On its own, this may seem insignificant, but when combined with other conscious choices about how to manage the fit between work and the other parts of their lives over time, it was the difference between satisfaction and being overwhelmed.

But we tend to dismiss and undervalue the power of small choices and actions, no matter how great they make us feel. As I researched the *Tweak It* practice, I'd ask people to share the tweaks that were most meaningful to them. Inevitably, almost to a person, they'd preface their response with "This is going to sound stupid, but…" or "It's pretty mundane, but…" No matter how valuable that small step had been, they'd minimize it. Here are a few examples of powerful tweaks people shared that resulted in a measureable improvement on their stress level, relationships, health, productivity, creativity, and/or focus:

"This is going to sound so stupid, but whenever I go to the mailbox and my *US* magazine arrives, I always sit down for an hour and read it."

"This might sound silly, but just getting a chance to braid my daughter's hair before she gets on the bus, even one day a week, means so much to both of us."

"This isn't going to sound like much, but when my husband was sick I was assigned a parking space next to the building, which really helped if I had to run back home midday for some reason."

"It's not a big deal but whenever I have a client lunch I leave my phone in my office, so that I don't check it and can concentrate on being fully present with the person I'm meeting with."

Why do we underplay the impact of these small yet mighty tweaks? Perhaps it's because the popular expert advice about how to manage work and life often encourages more radical solutions like working four hours a week, getting rid of work schedules altogether, or striking out on your own. For some, this "big change" advice is going to sound inspirational, aspirational, and reasonable. But it neglects the rest of us. *Tweak It* shifts the focus beyond the large and overwhelming change, and helps you identify, bundle, and magnify the collective force of the small manageable steps that you choose to make.[4]

Not surprisingly, employers also benefit when employees are encouraged to create a solid day-to-day work+life fit foundation where what matters to them happens on a regular basis.[5] From working with tens of thousands of employees and hundreds of employers, I've discovered that the real reason most people disengage from, underperform in, or quit their jobs is an accumulation of small frustrations. They miss tucking their child into bed one too many times; they get reprimanded for staying home with their child on a snow day; they can't get to the dry cleaner before closing, go on a date, attend friends' birthday parties, or get to the gym. Each of these seemingly insignificant disappointments adds up, until the dam bursts. And they are all avoidable if everyone has the tools and flexibility to make subtle, barely noticeable shifts in how, when, or where they work and manage their lives.

PAYOFF #3: YOU'LL MASTER TECHNOLOGY TO ACHIEVE YOUR GOALS, BECAUSE TECHNOLOGY IS NOT GOING AWAY.

"Technology is the problem. I can't get away from my smartphone, my iPad, my computer." I hear some version of this frustration practically every time I walk into a client site and start talking to people about their challenges managing their work and life.[6] And while I empathize, my ultimate reaction is "Yes, now what are you going to do about it?"

Technology is another example of how we're stuck in the 1960s instead of adapting to modern reality. Too many of us are still waiting for our employer to say, "Okay, everyone turn off your cell phones and don't check e-mail." Companies have tried this approach with little success with programs such as e-mail-free Fridays. Why? Because in a 24/7 global economy inevitably someone somewhere is going to have to correspond with another person in order to service a client or address an important issue during that "technology blackout" period.

Externally mandated, across-the-board rules governing the use of technology on and off the job generally do not work. So it's time to switch our thinking and make technology the solution that *we* manage, and not the problem that controls us until someone says, "Turn it off."[7] The *Tweak It* practice tackles this challenge in two ways:

First, a number of experts in the *Tweak It* Inspiration section of the book offer great advice on small, very doable ways that you can put boundaries around technology.

Second, the *Tweak It* online community harnesses technology and makes it work *for* you. The mobile app lets you access your Tweaks of the Week from your mobile device and check them regularly to make sure you are on track. By monitoring your progress live, you are more likely to achieve your goal for the week. The *Tweak It* Facebook, YouTube, and Twitter pages allow you to share with the online community what worked and what didn't. Get inspiration from others about what they're doing.

Technology, with its insatiable demands for connectedness, is not going away. And no one is ever going to be able to tell you when to turn it off. But a big payoff of *Tweak It* is it puts you in control and makes technology work for you, not against you.

Weighing the price versus the payoffs of Tweak It

What's the final tally? One price versus at least three major, life-changing payoffs from the *Tweak It* practice:

Prices of Tweak It	*Payoffs of* Tweak It
✓ You commit to doing the practice as consistently as possible (but not perfectly).	✓ You're more likely to keep your job and love your life in a very competitive, rapidly changing global economy.
	✓ You'll value and harness the power of the small, manageable activities and priorities that build your everyday foundation of well-being and order without being overwhelmed.
	✓ You'll master technology to achieve the goals *you* want, because technology is not going away.

When we conduct the prices/payoffs exercise with managers to help them see the benefits of supporting more work flexibility, my business partner, Donna Miller, closes out the session by asking managers, "In which column do you want to live—prices or payoffs?" Inevitably the benefits in the payoffs column outweigh the prices listed, and overwhelmingly, they choose payoffs. I hope you'll want to choose the payoffs column, too.

What's Next:

You are ready to be introduced to the *Tweak It* practice. We'll start with a general overview.

How do you *Tweak It*?

Step Away from the Screen

Once or twice a week, I go into a chapel in New York City and I'll meditate for five or ten minutes. It's important to step away, especially in today's workplace where the computer is so demanding. The computer doesn't sort things out easily for us, so we have to be the sorting mechanism. You're being paid to be proactive, and you need to stay on top and manage the work that is constantly coming at you.

—Rick Hamlin, executive editor of *Guideposts* magazine

Find a Common Interest, Find a Date

One of my clients is into art. He loves to paint, does ceramics, and also loves music. He was painting and listening to music, but he wasn't doing anything that would allow him to engage with

(continued)

---

others. I had him do a search on Meetup.com to find either art groups or music groups to join. He ended up meeting the woman who is now his fiancée through a music group. She's a recording artist and she plays music as well, so it was an easy blend, a good connection between the two of them.

—Thomas Edward, founder of The Professional
Wingman online dating service

How do you *Tweak It*?

Give a Gift and a Skill

My friend, John, is an architect and has always played the harmonica. One day, he decided to buy harmonicas and offer them to homeless folks in Seattle where he lives. Not only that, but he also offered to give them a quick lesson. I thought this was so cool, because it wasn't just about giving someone a thing, but about really giving him a new skill. A skill that might cheer them up and just be a way to pass the time and bring joy to other people, but maybe help economically if they played the harmonica and people gave them money. It was a gift that worked on so many levels—and couldn't fail to bring joy.

—Courtney Martin, author of *Do It Anyway:*
The New Generation of Activists

Let Video Show the World Who You Are

A former client was dead set against creating videos of herself online. She is a marital and family therapist and she just thought,

(continued)

Oh that's unprofessional and I'm not going to look good. I tried to convince her that it's the ultimate calling card because when people vet you, they want to see how you sound, how you look, and how you think. She recently sent me an e-mail to say that I was right. She'd invested in good lighting and camera people and created a few videos on YouTube. She has had wonderful professional opportunities come to her because of them.

—Carley Knobloch, founder of Digitwirl™.

TWEAK IT
THE PRACTICE

Chapter 3

Tweak It *Practice—*
An Overview

Tweak It will transform you into a work+life fit natural. You'll learn their secrets and join the 10 to 15 percent of the population who've figured out how to make what matters to them happen regularly in a modern, hectic world.

A natural is like the five-year-old kid in your neighborhood who jumped on a two-wheel bike and just started riding. No training wheels. No instruction. But chances are you weren't that kid. Bike riding wasn't intuitive. Success meant practice and thinking about what you were doing. You needed an extra set of wheels and someone to help you along before it became second nature.

Maybe you needed extra help for a short time, or perhaps (like me) you had training wheels for months. And, even then, you took them on and off several times before finally fumbling your way to that glorious day when you rode off on your own.

Today, it's the same with work and life. Many of us struggle. The three phases of the *Tweak It* practice take what's second nature for the work+life fit naturals and show you how to put their secrets of success into action. It's the set of training wheels, the explanation, the cheering section, and the supportive hand that helps you build a foundation of well-being and order in your life, one small step at a time. The three phases of the *Tweak It* practice are:

- Phase 1: Get Started
- Phase 2: Pick Your Unique Tweaks of the Week
- Phase 3: Review Your *Tweak It* Practice and Revise

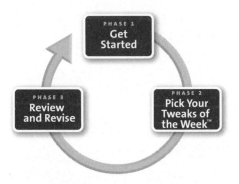

In this chapter, you'll be introduced to an overview of all of the practice phases. Then, the phases will each be discussed in more detail in chapters 4 to 6. Let's begin with Phase 1.

Phase 1: Get Started. The heaviest lifting in the *Tweak It* practice (which isn't that heavy) takes place in the steps that get you started. Once you've laid a solid foundation, you don't have to repeat these steps unless you want to later. They include:

- **Step 1: Create a complete picture, or *Tweak It* snapshot, of your work+life fit.** Bring the activities and priorities at work together with the activities and priorities in your personal life into one complete picture, or *Tweak It* snapshot. No longer will you think about and run these two pieces of your life separately. You will see them as a whole. This initial *Tweak It* snapshot becomes the starting point that you'll adjust weekly.

- **Step 2: Pick a simple calendar and priority list system to track and monitor the activities and priorities that make up your *Tweak It* snapshot.** You'll choose some combination of a simple calendar and priority list system to keep track of the small weekly changes you're going to make to your *Tweak It* snapshot. Whether it's Google Calendar, Outlook, iCalendar, a paper notebook, or an Excel spreadsheet, you'll choose the system that's easiest for you to work with.

- **Step 3: Decide what you want success to look like.** Before you begin, think about how you will know the *Tweak It* practice is helping you. Define success.

- **Step 4: Choose your standard tweaks, or the small activities and priorities, that will stay the same every week.** Some of your small, everyday *Tweak It* activities and priorities won't change week to week, whether it's when you exercise, see a friend, volunteer, and so on. These standard tweaks will form the consistent base of your *Tweak It* snapshot around which you'll tweak other to-dos that do shift as your life changes. These tweaks may include getting to the gym two times a week, having a date night with your partner, or meeting a friend for lunch each Saturday.

Once you've finished the "get started" steps, you'll have built the foundation for a successful *Tweak It* practice. The *Tweak It* snapshot of the actions and priorities in your work and life is complete. You have a simple tracking system, you've defined success, and identified your standard tweaks. You're ready to move on to the active Tweaks of the Week phase of the practice. This is where finding time every day for what matters to you becomes part of your weekly routine.

Phase 2: Pick Your Unique Tweaks of the Week. This dynamic weekly phase of the practice should take no more than thirty minutes. The amount of effort will depend upon how much time you want to spend figuring out which small activities and priorities matter most to you over the next seven days. You begin with a review.

- **Step 1: Review your *Tweak It* snapshot from the previous week.** Review the standard and unique Tweaks of the Week you chose for the prior week. Look at your *Tweak It* snapshot calendar and priority list. What actions and priorities happened, what didn't, and why? What's missing? What activities and priorities do you wish happened more frequently? What do you want to happen less often?
- **Step 2: Select your unique Tweaks of the Week.** Depending upon how you answered the questions above in your review, choose the new unique tweaks you want to commit to for the coming week. For creative tweak ideas, check out the *Tweak It* Practice Stories in the

second section of the book (chapters 7–10), and the *Tweak It* Inspiration advice from the fifty-plus experts in the final section of the book (chapters 11–17). And don't forget the tips and strategies we'll share with each other in the *Tweak It* online community (www.tweakittogether.com).

• **Step 3: Put your tweaks into your calendar and priority list, then communicate and collaborate to make them happen.** Pick the best day and time for each tweak based on your work commitments for the coming week. What's set in stone? What can you change? How much flexibility do you have to work differently? Coordinate and communicate with your family, friends, coworkers, and boss as needed. Input your tweaks into your *Tweak It* snapshot calendar and priority list. Check your system frequently and use the *Tweak It* online community and mobile app for support and to track your progress throughout the week.

The active Tweaks of the Week phase of the practice is where you will spend most of your time; however, make it a point to periodically step back and take stock. In Phase 3, you'll want to conduct an overall review of the *Tweak It* practice and make adjustments.

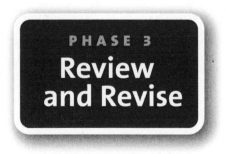

Phase 3: Review Your *Tweak It* Practice and Revise. Whether it's every three months, every six months, or once a year, take a few extra minutes to review your longer-term goals as well as the overall *Tweak It* practice. Update and revise as needed.

What are your longer-term goals? How might those goals affect the tweaks you select weekly? For example, perhaps since you began the *Tweak It* practice, you've decided that you might want to start you own business in the next year. That will influence the small steps you will take going forward.

Does the calendar and priority list tracking system you're using to manage your *Tweak It* snapshot meet your needs? Do you want to add or remove activities and priorities from your standard tweaks? Does the way you measure success reflect what you want *Tweak It* to help you achieve? Do you need to change the time and day that you pick the unique Tweaks of the Week? Make the required adjustments and continue to *Tweak It*.

Summary: Tweak It *Practice at a Glance*

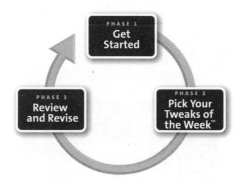

Tweak It translates the secrets of the work+life fit naturals into a simple practice that helps you find the time every day to make what matters to you happen. It's the extra support, the clear explanation, the cheering section, and the helping hand until the practice becomes second nature and part of your routine.

Read the following overview of the three phases of the *Tweak It* practice, then let's look at each phase in more detail in the following chapters.

PHASE 1: GET STARTED—ONCE-AND-DONE STEPS

- Create a complete picture, or *Tweak It* snapshot, of your work+life fit today, which are your current activities and priorities on and off the job.
- Pick a simple calendar and priority list system to manage and monitor the activities and priorities of your *Tweak It* snapshot weekly.
- Decide what you want success to look like.
- Choose any new standard tweaks, or small activities and priorities that you want to happen regularly every week.

PHASE 2: PICK YOUR UNIQUE TWEAKS OF THE WEEK— WEEKLY STEPS

- Review your *Tweak It* snapshot calendar and priority list from the previous week.
- Select the unique Tweaks of the Week you want to add for the next seven days.
- Put your tweaks into your *Tweak It* worksheet, snapshot calendar, and priority list, then communicate and collaborate to make them happen.

PHASE 3: REVIEW YOUR TWEAK IT PRACTICE. REVISE—PERIODIC STEP

What's Next:

Let's begin with a more detailed look at how to get started in Phase 1 of the *Tweak It* practice.

Chapter 4

Tweak It
Phase 1—Get Started

To master any activity, you have to practice before it becomes a habit. But first you have to set up. To practice basketball, you have to find a ball, some type of net, and a flat surface. To ride a two-wheeler, you need a working bike, a helmet, and a safe place to ride. The more time you spend making sure your basketball has enough air to bounce when you dribble and your bicycle stops when you apply the brakes, the more successful your practice will be and the more likely you are to master it.

It's the same with *Tweak It*. If you set up a strong, basic foundation, the active Tweaks of the Week phase of the practice in Phase 2 will be more effective, enjoyable, and easier. The first step is to bring all of the pieces of your work and life together into one complete picture, or *Tweak It* snapshot.

Step 1: Create a complete picture, or Tweak It *snapshot, of all the parts of your work+life fit, which are the activities and priorities in which you currently engage on and off the job.*

The first secret of the work+life fit naturals that I discovered in my research was that they see their lives as a whole picture. They don't separate what they are doing at work from the other parts of their lives that matter to them. In their minds and on paper (or with technology) they manage it all as one.

While each part of their lives doesn't get equal attention all the time, they decide what they will and will not do by thinking about how all of the pieces fit together. For example, it's unlikely that a natural would decide to go on a business trip only to discover later that she'll be away for her son's science fair. Because she keeps the whole picture of what's going on in her life at the top of her mind, she'll either try to reschedule the trip, or go away but plan something special in advance with her son to make up for missing the fair.

So what do the rest of us do? My research shows that most of us see our work and the other parts of our lives as separate. We manage our everyday choices from that split perspective, if we manage them at all. This false separation, mentally and on paper, is why I hear so many stories of people struggling to make even the most basic parts of their lives happen on a regular basis. Managing work and life in our modern, hectic world is not second nature to most of us, which is why we need to write down, "Schedule dinner with my high school friend, Jim," "Do nothing this afternoon," or "Get my physical," or it doesn't happen.

As I explained in the Introduction, my initial attempts to share the everyday secrets of the work+life fit naturals met with pushback as people would swear to me, "But I already do that and I am still overwhelmed." The problem was, and still is, that we *think* that we actively manage our work and life so that what matters to us happens every day, but in practice we don't. Perception doesn't match reality for most of us, but I needed proof to get past the resistance.

As I explained in the introduction, for the next few months I asked every group that I presented to if they would complete a short presession survey. A total of 242 working adults from eight different industries (for example, tax, technology, higher education, consumer products, and so on) answered the questions.

The findings confirmed my suspicions. To the statement "On average, I actively manage my work and personal to-dos . . . ," 75 percent of the respondents said "daily" or "weekly." In other words, most of them honestly believed that they were already doing what they needed to do to fit all the parts of their life together. However, the gap between perception and reality became clear with the next question. To the statement "I keep a calendar with all of my work and personal to-dos in one place," only 40 percent said, "always." Less than half were making their everyday decisions about what matters based on a complete picture of what they were trying to accomplish on and off the job.

Because most of us don't consistently see and track our work and life in one place, your first step of the practice is to pull all of the pieces together and create a complete picture, or *Tweak It* snapshot, of your work+life fit today. These are the activities and priorities you are currently doing on and off the job. Then in Step 2, you're going to set up a calendar and priority list system to track and monitor your *Tweak It* snapshot as it changes each week.

Step 2: Pick a simple calendar and priority list system to manage and monitor your Tweak It *snapshot.*

For years, popular productivity systems like FranklinCovey have tried to convince us to track our work and personal activities and priorities in one place. But, as my research proved, the message didn't get through.

In the 1960s, when the boundaries between work and the other parts of our lives were much more clear and rigid, perhaps we didn't need a combined system to get things done. Not anymore. This is the second secret of the work+life fit naturals that I discovered: a simple calendar and priority list tracking system is a must.

Here's an example of how you benefit from keeping your work and personal goals and priorities in one *Tweak It* snapshot: Your team at work plans the launch of a new product and schedules a series of critical meetings. One of the proposed dates is Thursday, April 4. When you look at the calendar and priority list that give you a complete *Tweak It* snapshot, you see that's the day of your best friend's birthday. Because she lives two hours away, you wanted to work from home in order to make it to her party in time. You suggest another day and the team agrees. Everyone's happy.

Conversely, *not* having a combined calendar and priority list system leads to unnecessary stress and disappointment. When the team proposes Thursday, April 4, you look at your work calendar. It says you are clear that day. The group sets the meeting schedule. But two months later on April 2, your friend calls to remind you, "Don't forget about my birthday party on Thursday," and you realize there's a conflict. It's too hard to reschedule the meeting, so you're late for the party because you can't get home in time. You and your friend are disappointed. No one is happy.

Common *Tweak It* monitoring systems: Most people use some type of simple combination of a calendar and a priority list. How that works is going to depend upon the system that your workplace uses and how comfortable you are sharing your personal activities and priorities in it. If you go to the *Tweak It* community site, you'll see explanations and links to various types of tracking systems; however, here are the few I've seen used most regularly:

- **Google Calendar:** This is the system that I use. I can have one separate personal calendar and one separate work calendar. But what

I like is that I'm able to display them together or individually. Not only is the Google Calendar system easy, I can access it anywhere. And I can allow other people to have access to specific calendars as well. I also use Behance's Action Method online system to track my projects and priorities, both personal and professional. Together they form my *Tweak It* snapshot.

• **Outlook for both work and personal activities and tasks:** This is what many people who work inside of traditional organizations use. Depending upon their level of comfort, some people may also create individual work and personal calendars in their Outlook that they control separately but display together.

• **Outlook with work to-dos, and a separate personal calendar and list kept on the desk or open in another window:** This combination of a work and personal calendar and to-do list monitored simultaneously is another alternative that I've seen used by people who really don't want their personal activities and priorities in their work system at all. Instead, they keep their personal calendar/list on the desk or open online (for example, with Google Calendar) and refer to it often.

I've also met people who use an Excel spreadsheet to track what they want to get done personally and professionally in a week. The options are endless. Recently, everyday tech guru Carley Knobloch, founder of Digit-wirl, a web show about making tech actually work for you, told me about Cozi.com, a mobile app of calendars and lists for families. Another combination used by Apple fans is iCalendar and the list app called Remember the Milk™.

Here's an example of the Tweaks of the Week that a brand manager named Lisa input into her *Tweak It* snapshot calendar and priority list. You will hear more about Lisa's *Tweak It* story and also follow Jeff, Denise, and Pete to see how their tweaks changed over a four-week period in chapters 7–10.

Monday	Tuesday	Wednesday	Thursday	Friday	Saturday	Sunday
Work 8:00 a.m. to 6:00 p.m. in office	Work 8:00 a.m. to 6:00 p.m. in office	Work 8:00 a.m. to 6:00 p.m. in office	Work 8:00 a.m. to 6:00 p.m. from home; overseas call/meeting coverage	Work 8:00 a.m. to 6:00 p.m. in office		
8:00 a.m.: Pick Tweaks of the Week			8:30 a.m.: Set up travel account		8:00 a.m.: Time with Jack	8:00 a.m.: Subscribe to travel info
11:30 a.m.: Lunch/walk	12:30 p.m.: Lunch/walk			1:00 p.m.: Lunch/walk	2:00 p.m.: Recipe/meal planning 3:00 p.m.: Do nothing	
8:00 p.m.: Chloe	7:00 p.m.: Family dinner 8:00 p.m.: Chloe 8:30 p.m.: Do nothing 9:30 p.m.: Time with Jack	8:00 p.m.: Chloe	8:00 p.m.: Chloe	8:00 p.m.: Chloe		6:00 p.m.: Family dinner/travel date planning

Priority List

✓ Take stairs at work
✓ Listen to Luke more, talk less
✓ Drink more water

Again, be sure to check out and share calendar and priority list system ideas on the *Tweak It* community. Be creative. Find the system that's going to be easiest for you to monitor, and adjust your *Tweak It* snapshot each week.

At this point in Phase 1 of the *Tweak It* practice, you've pulled all of the activities and priorities in your work and life into one complete picture, or *Tweak It* snapshot. You've set up a calendar and priority list system to track the changes you're going to make to your *Tweak It* snapshot weekly. Now it's time to lay the next piece of your foundation and think about what success with the *Tweak It* practice will look like for you.

Your *Tweak It* worksheet

Take a few minutes to either print out a *Tweak It* worksheet (PDF) from the online community, or use a notebook to record your work in the following steps of the practice.

Step 3: Decide what success will look like.

"How will I know the *Tweak It* practice is working?" It's an important question to answer before you begin. If you determine what you want success to look like up front, and periodically monitor your progress in Phase 3, you'll stay motivated when *Tweak It* becomes a habit that you want to sustain.

That picture of success will look different for each of us, and may include some of the following:

There's more satisfaction, contentment, and order in the areas of life that are most important to you right now. Each of us must define for ourselves what satisfaction, contentment, and order looks and feels like at a given point in time. What activities am I doing more often and less often because of the *Tweak It* practice? Am I feeling different? More content? Less stressed? More connected with those I love? Healthier?

What tangible changes have taken place? Are you more financially sound? More organized?

You've completed the *Tweak It* practice consistently week after week. In today's modern, ever-changing work and life reality, there's no answer or right way to fit it all together. Circumstances change constantly; therefore, you only can commit to a consistent practice that helps you to make decisions that are right for you now.

For example, two people will follow the *Tweak It* practice for a year. Over that fifty-two-week period, each person will focus on different personal and professional tweaks at different times. One person makes health and wellness a priority for a few months, while the other will put more emphasis on his finances and caregiving responsibilities. The weekly tweaks they need to build a foundation of well-being and order may be completely different, but the one thing they have in common is the *Tweak It* practice to guide their choices in the right direction. The more often they commit to a deliberate, decision-making practice, the more consistently successful they will be.

You've moved beyond the limitations and judgments of work/ life balance. As we discussed in the Introduction, one of the seven truths of work and life in our modern, hectic world is that there is no balance. One way to measure the success of the *Tweak It* practice over time is to move beyond the limits of balance.[1] What does that look like?

• **You no longer believe the goal is a 50-50 split between work and the other parts of your life that *balance* suggests.** In today's competitive, service-oriented global economy there are very few jobs where a consistent amount of work will always be done on particular days and within certain hours. Yes, fifteen years ago, you could count on a pretty reliable schedule. And you could walk out the door at the end of the day and not have to reconnect to work until you walked back in. No longer. To find a fit that works for you and your job, *Tweak It* acknowledges this inherent workflow inconsistency and connectivity. It helps you to create boundaries around technology and to accommodate the inevitable ebbs and flows at work and at home.

• **You talk about what you could have with *Tweak It* versus what you don't have with work/life balance.** Balance is almost always discussed in the negative—"I don't have balance," or "I am out of balance"—but with *Tweak It* . . .

• **You stay focused on solutions and not the problem.** *Tweak It* gives you the power to make deliberate, small adjustments in the way you work and manage your life, and in the process . . .

• **You realize that we all have different activities and priorities that matter to us.** *Balance* assumes we're all the same. We're not. At any given time, we all have a completely unique set of work and *personal* circumstances to tweak in a week. For Kate, who's on the steep learning curve of a new job and works long hours, getting to the gym and seeing her friends every couple of weeks is enough. But for Mark, three days a week mentoring new salespeople is perfect, because he can delay retirement for two years and see his grandchildren more.

• **You understand that there is no right answer, only what works for you and your job.** *Balance* implies that there's a right answer. There isn't. If the reality on and off the job for each of us is completely unique, then there's never going to be a right way or balance. I've met an investment manager who runs a small not-for-profit on the side, an accountant who's a mom and a competitive ballroom dancer, and an entrepreneur who gets home twice a week for dinner with his kids and tries to slip in time to surf during his eighty-hour workweek. They were able to tweak their activities and priorities in a way that *works for them in the context* of these unique personal and professional realities. No one is right. No one is wrong.

• **You are less judgmental of yourself and of others.** Because with *Tweak It* there is no right answer, we can give each other and ourselves a break. There's a lot of judgment attached to balance, in terms of who's perceived to have it and who doesn't. We have no idea what's going on in someone else's life or in their job. Instead of judging, we can share *Tweak It* strategies from the book and in the *Tweak It* community at www .tweakittogether.com. "How does an entrepreneur get home for dinner and surf?" "How do you manage investments and run a not-for-profit?" "How does a mother work as an accountant and find time to be a ballroom dancer?" Rather than judging, we can inspire.

• **You feel less unproductive guilt.** There's a lot of guilt with balance, especially if you feel you don't have it. If different activities and priorities on and off the job matter to us, then there should be no (or at least less) guilt.

• **You're prepared for and can adapt to unexpected periods of more work and less life, and vice versa.** Everyday work and life flexibility requires adapting to unexpected shifts in the amount of attention you have to devote to work and life without feeling you are out of balance. If an important, unexpected project has to be completed and you're supposed to leave early that day at 4 p.m., occasionally step to the plate and stay later at work without complaint. The unanticipated will happen.

In summary, you'll know that the *Tweak It* practice is helping you find time for what uniquely matters to you when you've moved beyond the limits of balance, because you will:

• see solutions, rather than limitations;
• know we're all different;
• realize there's no right answer;
• stop judging yourself and others;
• lose the guilt; and
• embrace and plan for the ebb and flow of work and life.

If any or all of the above is true for you, then you are making progress with *Tweak It*.

You're able to celebrate when you achieve 70 percent of your

standard and unique Tweaks of the Week because the goal is not perfection. Voltaire was right when he said, "The perfect is the enemy of the good." And from my experience helping tens of thousands of people manage the way work fits into their lives over the past two decades, perfection is our worst adversary. This is especially true for high-achievers.

Karen attended one of my workshops. As we went around the room sharing the top-three small changes the group wanted to incorporate into their work+life fit for the week, it was Karen's turn. Obviously frustrated, she said, "I just can't seem to get to the gym." I responded, "Okay, let's look at what's going on."

Karen explained that she had two small children, worked part-time, and was going to school at night, "and I really want to get to the gym because I feel so much better when I exercise." She had a lot on her plate, but I thought there had to be some way she could find a way to stay in shape. So I asked her to share what she'd tried to do that hadn't succeeded. She continued, "Well, my goal is to get to the gym five days a week and work out for two hours. And I can't seem to get there more than two, maybe three, days a week. I'm very frustrated."

I was confused, and I could see the other people in the group were grappling with how to help Karen because to all of us, getting to the gym at least twice maybe three times a week for two hours was fantastic considering everything else Karen was doing.

But she was visibly struggling and I wanted to honor that. I decided that there had to be more going on, and I asked Karen, "Why does it have to be five days a week for two hours?"

She said with a straight face, "Because when I was a professional ballet dancer, I worked out every day for hours. Two hours five days a week is nothing, but I can't seem to make it happen."

Now I understood. Karen had set her bar of success too high for the circumstances she was trying to manage at the moment. "What if," I replied, "you reset your goal to one that would be more realistic given your current circumstances? And then, give yourself credit when you achieve even

70 percent of what you wanted to do. Getting to the gym twice a week for two hours is better than not going at all. The weeks you can get there three, even four, times are wonderful but shouldn't be the goal."

Her face visibly relaxed and she smiled. "Yes, using my professional ballet days before I had children or went to school as my gauge of success doesn't make a lot of sense."

And one woman in the group laughed, "If I got to the gym twice a week for two hours, I'd think I was an Olympic athlete!"

Can you relate to Karen? I can sometimes, and I've met thousand of wonderful, thoughtful people just like her. Their common challenge is that they've set the bar so high for their personal and professional goals that they are always falling short and giving up in frustration. No mortal living in a world of competing, ever-changing work and personal priorities is going to get it 100 percent right every time.

There was a time when I was more like Karen, but as I studied how the work+life fit naturals operated, I realized that I needed to give myself a break. They didn't see failure when an activity or event didn't happen. They felt good about accomplishing most of what they wanted to do and moved on. If you are achieving 70 percent of your Twcaks of the Week most of the time, then you should be satisfied with your *Tweak It* progress.

You manage your time and energy for the highest return. Does this sound familiar? "On paper, I still have the same number of hours I always did to get things done, but I just don't have the energy. I am going to hit the wall." As Laura Vanderkam points out in her book *168 Hours*, we have twenty-four hours a day, seven days a week, to complete everything we need to accomplish on and off the job.[2] But then another expert, Tony Schwartz, says that you should "Manage Your Energy, Not Your Time," in the classic 2007 article he coauthored with Catherine McCarthy for the *Harvard Business Review*.[3] Is it time? Is it energy? Actually, it's both.

This focus on time *and* energy is another new modern mind-set shift we need to make. "Time management" and "Productivity" are manufacturing-era concepts. In fact, experts can trace the earliest time-management systems in the United States as far back as Benjamin Franklin.[4] These time- and productivity-tracking formulas made sense when the goal was to produce as many widgets as possible in a fixed amount of time or when you got paid and promoted for the number of hours you worked.

But today, we aren't producing widgets. We're rewarded for "adding value," which means offering something above and beyond what's expected that makes the product or service you are providing more uniquely valuable. It means bringing the best of yourself to the table personally and professionally as often as you can. You do this by focusing on tweaks that give you the highest time/energy return, and asking for help with or letting go of those that don't return as much or simply drain you.

For example, I don't like to cook. Creating a meal, gathering all of the ingredients, figuring out how to cook it, cooking it, serving it, worrying whether or not people like it, clearing the table and cleaning up, completely overwhelms any benefit I get from eating healthfully. The time taken up by the whole cooking process leaves me with less energy than when I started (in fact, I feel drained just writing about it). The time/ energy return for me is negative. So I keep weekly food preparation and delivery for my family as healthy, simple, and easy as possible. And often my babysitter, who loves to cook, prepares dinner. As a result, I have more time and energy for the parts of my work and life where I add more value because the time/energy return is positive. Such as writing this book. It's hard. It takes a lot of time, but I love it.

On the other hand, my friend Barbara loves to cook and entertain. The time/energy return for her is much higher and, therefore, worthwhile. All is right in her world after she's prepared and presented a good meal. In fact, my family actually cheers out loud when we are invited over to her house for dinner. On the other hand, she would never, ever want to write a book.

Part of the *Tweak It* practice involves estimating the time/energy return from each of the small, deliberate activities and priorities that you choose. *Tweak It* success happens when you consciously invest in key areas of your work and life where the energy you get back is worth more than the time it took to complete the task. You let go of or get help with as many of the activities as you can where the energy you get back is worth less than the time invested. For example, continue to walk with your partner twice a week because, while it takes sixty minutes, you feel reenergized afterward. On the other hand, if after spending four hours cleaning your house, you are so drained that you have nothing left for the rest of the day, consider getting your family or someone else to help you.

Finally, you feel you are more in control of your decisions. A few months ago I attended a workshop facilitated by Geneen Roth, the author of *Women Food and God.*[5] During her session, she used a great analogy to describe how little control we feel we have over what happens in our lives: "It's as if each morning someone delivers a memo outlining all of the things we need to do for the day, and we just sigh and say, 'Fine,' as if we have no control." It doesn't have to be this way.

You will know the *Tweak It* practice is working when you stop passively letting your work and life just happen and begin to take charge and create the reality you want. You decide consciously whether to say yes or no to conflicting opportunities and responsibilities as they arise. You deliberately negotiate the seemingly endless everyday micro-trade-offs we all must make:

- Leave work a few minutes early to get to the gym, or prepare for a last-minute meeting?
- Work from home in the evening to catch up on e-mails, or meet a friend for coffee?
- Cover a coworker's shift, or shop for food for the week?
- Ask for overtime, or take your mother to the doctor?
- Catch up on paperwork, or read at your child's school?
- Go to a lunchtime networking event, or balance your checkbook?

Success is no longer feeling like you are a passive bystander following orders that someone else outlined in a memo. With *Tweak It* you are writing your own memo to accomplish what matters most to you.

Write down in your *Tweak It* worksheet what you want the *Tweak It* practice to help you achieve. Success can take many forms and needs to be defined by each of us. Here's a review of the potential benefits we just covered and that you may want to include:

- more satisfaction, contentment, and order in all parts of your life as the activities and priorities that matter to you are happening more consistently;
- consistently completing the *Tweak It* practice week after week;
- moving beyond the limitations and judgments of work/life balance;
- feeling good that you've achieved at least 70 percent of your standard and unique Tweaks of the Week, because the goal is not perfection;
- managing your time *and* energy for the highest return; and
- feeling you are more in control of your decisions.

Step 4: Choose the standard tweaks that will stay the same every week.

A tweak is either an activity that you do or a priority that you want to focus on. For example, "Call John to catch up and network" is an activity that goes into your calendar, while "Listen for opportunities to compliment my teenager" is a priority that you keep front and center on a list.

Some of these small activities and priorities will happen consistently week after week, or month after month. These are your standard tweaks. They include any regular action you are already doing as well as new ones you might want to add at the start of the *Tweak It* practice. Standard activities might be exercising, taking a class, making a meal, or going on a regular date night with your partner. Standard priorities could include "Turn off my technology when I am talking to someone."

Recurring standard tweaks that are already part of your *Tweak It* snapshot. For example, I already exercise for an hour five days every week on a pretty consistent schedule. I meditate for fifteen minutes five mornings a week, and go to the grocery store every Sunday. Those are my nonnegotiable, recurring tweaks that I try to complete 70 percent of the time each week. I also make it a priority to tell my husband I love him every morning when he leaves for work and hug my kids at least once a day. You may even have a standard time to check your personal budget, or have dinner with your best friend.

New standard tweaks you'd like to add to your *Tweak It* snapshot. Are there any small activities and priorities you'd like to add to your regular routine that aren't happening right now? Maybe you want to go to bed at a certain time or practice piano once a week. Perhaps you'd like to spend ten minutes with each of your children every day or eat lunch with your aging parent at least once a week.

Pick the *most important* new standard tweak. The day and time that you'll choose your Tweaks of the Week every seven days is your most important standard tweak. The time and day may vary a bit depending upon your schedule, but this tweak should be as consistent as possible so that it becomes part of your routine.

Tweak inspiration resources

Remember there are a number of resources to help you identify the standard tweaks you may want to add. There are the *Tweak It* Practice Stories (chapters 7–10) where you see how four people with very different jobs and lives—Lisa, Jeff, Denise, and Pete—make simple priorities and activities part of their weekly routines. And you can refer to the simple, get-started tips of the fifty-plus experts who specialize in the following areas that are found in the *Tweak It* Inspiration section (chapters 11–17):

Renew Tweaks
- ✓ Move Your Body
- ✓ Choose Healthy Food
- ✓ Prepare Healthy Meals
- ✓ Get More Sleep
- ✓ Learn to Meditate
- ✓ Do Nothing…Often
- ✓ Take a Vacation
- ✓ Celebrate Good Times
- ✓ Create, Dream, Escape
- ✓ Practice Your Faith
- ✓ Give Something Back
- ✓ Manage Tech Distraction

Career Tweaks
- ✓ Build Your Network
- ✓ Create Virtual You
- ✓ Update Your Skills
- ✓ Learn New Technologies
- ✓ Know Your "Type"
- ✓ For Younger Workers
- ✓ For Older Workers
- ✓ Plan a Career Break
- ✓ Find an Encore (Preretirement) Career
- ✓ Start Your Own Business

Money Tweaks
- ✓ Everyday Finances
- ✓ Retirement Savings
- ✓ College Savings

Connect Tweaks
- ✓ Loved Ones
- ✓ Friends
- ✓ Date
- ✓ Community

Connect with Kids Tweaks
- ✓ Kids under Thirteen Years
- ✓ Teens
- ✓ Just for Dads
- ✓ Nieces/Nephews
- ✓ Technology
- ✓ School
- ✓ College Planning
- ✓ SAT Prep

Caregiving Tweaks
- ✓ Elder Care—General
- ✓ Elder Care—with Siblings
- ✓ Child Care—Regular and Backup
- ✓ Summer Care

Maintenance Tweaks
- ✓ Your Health
- ✓ Your Personal Appearance
- ✓ Your Car
- ✓ Your House—Get Organized
- ✓ Your House—Clean It Yourself
- ✓ Your House—Hire Cleaning Help
- ✓ Your House—Maintain It

Once you've identified your existing and new standard tweaks, list them in your *Tweak It* worksheet so that you can refer to them easily each week. Here's what the list of my standard tweaks looks like:

Standard Tweaks	Action or Priority
Select Tweaks of the Week	Action
Exercise	Action
Meditate	Action
Grocery-shop	Action
Connect with my husband at least once during the workday	Priority
Find ten minutes of uninterrupted time with each of the kids	Priority

Tweak It *Phase 1—Get Started Summary:*

Success in choosing your unique Tweaks of the Week in Phase 2 will be simpler and more enjoyable if you spend time to setting up the basics of the practice in Phase 1. These basics include:

- Step 1: Create a complete picture, or *Tweak It* snapshot, that pulls together all the activities and priorities that are happening in your work and life into one place. This is the first secret of the work+life fit naturals.
- Step 2: Pick a simple calendar and priority list system to manage and monitor your *Tweak It* snapshot as a complete picture. This is the second secret of the work+life fit naturals.
- Step 3: Decide what you want success to look like. It will be different for all of us. Do you want to feel less stressed? More connected to your friends and family? More organized? Healthier?

- Step 4: Choose your standard tweaks—small weekly activities and priorities—that will stay the same every week. They might include playing the piano twice a week, calling your parents, or picking out your clothes for the next day.

What's Next:

Now that you've completed Phase 1, you are ready to take a deeper dive into Phase 2 and actively pick your unique Tweaks of the Week every seven days.

How do you *Tweak It?*

Mindfully Meditate Your Way to Wellness

I have something called tinnitus, which is a condition that causes me to hear a constant loud, high-pitched ringing in my head. When it first happened to me, it was a horrible, horrible thing for months. I started to explore all sorts of different ways to deal with it, because even with modern medicine, there's no cure. There are all sorts of complementary things that you can try, and I've tried all of them. Most of the time they don't work. People tell you either learn to live with it or suffer horribly for the rest of your life.

That led me to explore using mindfulness as a way to step back from this and be able to refocus away from it. I gained a much bigger sense of equanimity around the idea that this is not going to kill me. It's a sound like every other sound. It's always there, but I don't have to focus on it. I don't have to experience it as pain or anxiety or whatever it is. It has been a long process and I go up and down. But those two things and a daily mindfulness practice have allowed me to go through each day reasonably comfortably now.

—Jonathan Fields, author of *Uncertainty: Turning Fear and Doubt into Fuel for Brilliance*

How do you *Tweak It?*

Power of "I Get To…"

A few years ago, a woman who is a minister inspired me to use the phrase "I get to." When I'm leaving for carpool, I don't say, "I have to leave for carpool," but "I get to leave for carpool." Or, "I get to take my son to soccer practice tonight." It totally changes your perspective. It reminds us of why we had these children—because we wanted them and we love them.

—Amy McCready, author of *If I Have to Tell You One More Time…: The Revolutionary Program That Gets Your Kids to Listen without Nagging, Reminding, or Yelling*

Make a Date with a Friend

My closest friend moved away. We used to work together. We saw each other on a daily basis. Now, she lives in another state, but we speak to each other almost every day, even if it is briefly. We get together every couple of months. It can be hard to pull yourself away from your work, but before the holidays she was in town and we met at a museum in the city. Those are the kinds of memories that keep the relationship going.

—Irene Levine, PhD, author of *Best Friends Forever: Surviving a Breakup with Your Best Friend*

Chapter 5

Tweak It *Phase 2—Pick Your Tweaks of the Week*

You've laid the groundwork for success in Phase 1. Now you are ready to start the active Tweaks of the Week phase, the *Tweak It* practice. It should take you no more than thirty minutes a week, depending upon how much effort you want to put into picking the unique activities and priorities you want to accomplish over the next seven days.

The steps in Phase 2 were inspired by the last two secrets of the work+life fit naturals that I discovered in my research. It turns out that the naturals instinctively maintain satisfaction, well-being, and order in their work and lives by:

- regularly asking themselves the question, "What do I want in my work and life?" (often unconsciously); and

- Intuitively making small, deliberate choices to close the gap whenever they see a mismatch between what they want to happen and what's actually happening.

For example, it's unlikely that a work+life fit natural realizes at the end of the year she has ten days of vacation left and no time to take it. Throughout the year, she monitors when she feels that she needs to recharge and get away. Then she dedicates the time required to budget, plan, and schedule a trip, even if it's just for a long weekend. She is consistent and deliberate about finding time every day for the small activities and priorities that are important to her, and that includes days off when she needs them.

What do the rest of us do? My research found that most of us never reflect on what we want, and almost no one closes the gaps between desire and reality when they appear. Let's go back to the brief survey I mentioned earlier that 242 working adults in eight diverse industry groups completed before my work+life fit presentations.

To the statement "On average, I set time aside to reflect on and to answer the question, 'What do I want in my work and life?'" only 26 percent responded yes "daily" or "weekly." But only 15 percent of the same group responded "always" to the statement "When there's a mismatch between what I want and my current work and life reality, I consciously make adjustments to close the gap." In other words, only a quarter of the 242 working adults I surveyed said that they regularly reflected on what they wanted in their work and life, and fewer than two in ten always took action to make what they wanted happen. Fifteen percent, or almost no one. Not a very optimistic, self-motivated picture.

This is why the active weekly Tweaks of the Week practice is so important. It takes what's second nature to the work+life fit naturals and makes it understandable and doable for the rest of us. It asks you to sit down once a week and deliberately ask yourself, "What do I want in my work and life?" or in other words, what activities and priorities are missing from the

Tweak It snapshot you created in Phase 1 and now adjust each week. Then, when you see a mismatch between what you want to happen and what's actually happening in your *Tweak It* snapshot, it shows you how to choose the tweaks for that week to close the gap. Follow these steps long enough, and you can't help but experience the same sense of everyday contentment, satisfaction, and control that's second nature to the naturals. And, at some point, the process may even become a habit. Like riding a bike.

Here are the three simple steps you will complete each week:

- Step 1: Review the activities and priorities on and off the job in your *Tweak It* snapshot from the previous week.
- Step 2: Select your unique Tweaks of the Week for the next seven days.
- Step 3: Put your tweaks into your *Tweak It* snapshot calendar and priority list, then communicate and collaborate to make them happen.

Your *Tweak It* Worksheet

In you haven't already, take a few minutes to either print out a *Tweak It* worksheet (PDF) from the online community, or use a notebook to record your work in the following steps.

Step 1: Review your Tweak It *snapshot calendar and priority list from the previous week.*

Review the list of standard and unique tweaks you chose for the prior week in your *Tweak It* snapshot calendar and priority list.

How did you do with your Tweaks of the Week over the past seven days?

- **Did the tweaks you chose happen?** Yes, no, or perhaps a little of both.
- **If yes, why did they work?** How can you replicate that success?
- **Was there a net gain of energy versus the time invested to complete a particular small action or priority?** Remember, it may take an hour to meet your friend for a cup of coffee in the afternoon, but what was the payoff in terms of a renewed level of energy and focus? Was it greater than the hour of time invested? Chances are the answer is yes. Then that would be a net gain. Write that down to remind yourself.
- **If a tweak didn't happen, why? What could you do differently?** Sometimes we learn even more from our failures than from our successes. It's no different with your *Tweak It* practice. It's absolutely okay if you weren't able to make a particular activity or priority happen during the week.

The important thing is to reflect and learn from experience as you think about the next round of tweaks you're going to choose. Usually, the solution is relatively easy.

For example, you didn't review your insurance coverage on Thursday evening as you had planned because you started to watch television and lost track of time. The lesson learned for next time is to complete the planned tweak first, then watch television. If it was an important show, set the DVR to record it and watch when you are done. Or perhaps an unexpected project landed on your desk at the last minute and you missed the family dinner you had planned for that night. The lesson learned for the next time is check on the status of your projects with your boss earlier in the day, and schedule time to talk to her about being able to finish any last-minute projects from home later in the evening or early the next day.

Some weeks you may complete only half of your chosen tweaks. While that's a bit of a bummer, at least 50 percent of what mattered to you happened that week. That's 50 percent more than if you hadn't chosen any tweaks at all. Remember, your goal is 70 percent, not perfection. As I learned from the work+life fit naturals, there's always next time.

- **Celebrate progress! It keeps you going.** There will be weeks where you accomplish all of the tweaks that you've chosen and maybe more. Yes! Spend a few minutes enjoying how good it feels and what a difference those tweaks made in your sense of overall contentment, satisfaction, and order, personally and professionally. Hang on to that feeling and remember it on the weeks your tweak success rate might not be as high.

From this review process, you can begin to see patterns. What parts of your everyday work+life fit are easier to manage than others? Why? What could you learn from the small activities and priorities that seem to get done with ease, and those you struggle with? You are ready to pick your tweaks for the coming week.

Step 2: Select your unique Tweaks of the Week for the next seven days.

These are the new small activities and priorities you'll choose for the coming week based on your answers to the review you just completed. Remember:

- What is missing from my work and life?
- What's working well?
- What do I want more of?
- What do I want less of?

Get Inspired: Again, this is where you may want to refer to all of the terrific *Tweak It* resources for inspiration. See the unique Tweaks of the Week that four individuals with very different lives on and off the jobs chose in the *Tweak It* Practice Stories (chapters 7–10). Check out in chapters 11–17 how the fifty-plus *Tweak It* Inspiration experts suggest you get started in the following areas:

Renew Tweaks

✓ Move Your Body
✓ Choose Healthy Food
✓ Prepare Healthy Meals
✓ Get More Sleep
✓ Learn to Meditate
✓ Do Nothing…Often
✓ Take a Vacation
✓ Celebrate Good Times
✓ Create, Dream, Escape
✓ Practice Your Faith
✓ Give Something Back
✓ Manage Tech Distraction

Career Tweaks

✓ Build Your Network
✓ Create Virtual You
✓ Update Your Skills
✓ Learn New Technologies
✓ Know Your "Type"
✓ For Younger Workers
✓ For Older Workers
✓ Plan a Career Break
✓ Find an Encore (Preretirement) Career
✓ Start Your Own Business

Money Tweaks

✓ Everyday Finances
✓ Retirement Savings
✓ College Savings

Connect Tweaks

✓ Loved Ones
✓ Friends
✓ Date
✓ Community

Connect with Kids Tweaks

✓ Kids under Thirteen Years
✓ Teens
✓ Just for Dads
✓ Nieces/Nephews
✓ Technology
✓ School
✓ College Planning
✓ SAT Prep

Caregiving Tweaks

✓ Elder Care—General
✓ Elder Care—with Siblings
✓ Child Care—Regular and Backup
✓ Summer Care

Maintenance Tweaks

✓ Your Health
✓ Your Personal Appearance
✓ Your Car
✓ Your House—Get Organized
✓ Your House—Clean It Yourself
✓ Your House—Hire Cleaning Help
✓ Your House—Maintain It

And, last but not least, each week go to the *Tweak It* online community (www.tweakittogether.com). Not only will I share my Tweaks of the Week, but you can check out the Facebook page, Twitter stream, and YouTube channel to see what others are doing. And share the tweaks that are working for you.

Find power-combo tweaks that accomplish two or more goals at the same time. Some activities and priorities you may choose can accomplish many small goals at once. These are called power-combo tweaks, and they might include the following:

• A woman walks her dog for thirty minutes up and down the steep hills in her area and leaves her phone at home so she's not distracted. She exercises while managing technology.

• A senior leader of global HR for a Fortune 500 company takes Tae Kwon Do with his wife and his sons twice a week. He's spending time with his wife and children while he's exercising.

The number of unique Tweaks of the Week you pick will vary and change depending upon what's happening on and off the job over the next seven days. There is no right number of tweaks you should pick each week. To estimate your capacity for new tweaks during a particular seven-day period, look at what will happen at work and in the other parts of your life in your *Tweak It* snapshot calendar and priority list. Review your standard tweaks. What more can you realistically take on? Maybe you can manage only one new unique tweak during a particularly busy week; that's fine. After you get into a rhythm, you may find you can accomplish fifteen unique tweaks in a week.

Each seven-day period will be different. Maybe start by adding two or three unique tweaks in key areas the first week and see how it goes. If it's not too overwhelming, think about choosing more the next time. If that's too much, scale back for a couple of weeks.

Adapt the practice as your personal and professional circumstances change. The point is to experiment, adjust, celebrate success, and let go of what doesn't happen.

Repeating a unique tweak: You may find that you repeat a particularly valuable tweak week after week. For example, planning your meals for the week on Friday afternoon and shopping for your groceries on the way home from work. Or writing a post every Thursday for your new professional blog. At some point, in Phase 3, you may decide officially to turn those helpful ongoing activities or priorities into standard tweaks that become a permanent part of your *Tweak It* snapshot.

Select your unique Tweaks of the Week and add them to your list of standard tweaks in the worksheet. Here's an example of six standard tweaks and five unique tweaks for a particular week.

Standard Tweaks	Action or Priority
Pick Tweaks of the Week	Action
Meditate	Action
Grocery-shop	Action
Exercise	Action
Connect with my husband at least once during the workday	Priority
Find ten minutes of uninterrupted time with each of the kids	Priority

Unique Tweaks of the Week	Action or Priority
Plan to do nothing	Action
Set up LinkedIn profile	Action
Buy a set of headphones for my desk so that I can stand and move while I talk on the phone	Action
Schedule a night out with friends by sending everyone an e-mail	Action
Remember to use a calm voice with the kids	Priority

Now it's time to plan when and how you are going to make your standard and unique Tweaks of the Week happen and track your progress.

Step 3: Add the tweaks listed in your worksheet into your Tweak It *snapshot calendar and priority list. Communicate and collaborate to make them happen.*

You've chosen to complete a certain number of activities and priorities over the next seven days. What do you need to do to make those tweaks a reality, and how are you going to track your progress? Think about the people on and off the job whom you need to communicate and collaborate with. Start by answering the following questions:

- **What's happening at work this week?** What work needs to get done in the next seven days? What might come up at the last minute? When, where, and how do you need to do that work?
- **Can you adjust when, where, or how you can get that work done?** According to the 2011 Work+Life Fit Reality Check, the national survey of adults working full-time that we conduct every two years, 62 percent of respondents said that they had some type of day-to-day, or ad hoc, flexibility in when, where, or how they worked.[1] If you are part of the majority that has work flexibility, then use it to make your Tweaks of the Week happen. Arrive at work a little bit later in the morning so you can get to the gym. Leave a little bit earlier to update your skills by taking a class. Work from home one day so that you don't have to commute and can volunteer serving dinner at a local nursing home.

What if you are part of the 38 percent that don't have any flexibility in how, when, or where you work? Because the activities and priorities you've chosen are so small and manageable, you should be able to get them done in and around your set schedule for the next seven days. You just have to be a little more creative, organized, and deliberate.

- **What is happening in the other parts of your life?** Do your children have activities scheduled? What does your partner's schedule look like on and off the job? Is there flexibility with any of those commitments?

• **Choose the best date and time to complete your tweaks and input them into your *Tweak It* snapshot calendar and priority list.** Based on your answers to the questions above, choose the best dates and times to execute the small activities and priorities you've chosen to complete over the next seven days:

Standard Tweaks	Action or Priority	Target Date/Time
Pick Tweaks of the Week	Action	Sunday, 7:30 p.m.
Meditate	Action	Monday–Friday, 5:30 a.m.
Grocery-shop	Action	Sunday, 10:30 a.m.
Exercise	Action	Tuesday, 6:30 a.m.; Wednesday, 5:00 p.m.; Thursday, 5:00 p.m.; Friday, 6:30 a.m.; Saturday, 7:00 a.m.
Connect with my husband at least once during the workday	Priority	Every morning at least
Find ten minutes of uninterrupted time with each of the kids	Priority	Once a day at least

Unique Tweaks of the Week	Action or Priority	Target Date/Time
Plan to do nothing	Action	Saturday from 3:00 p.m. to 5:00 p.m.
Set up LinkedIn profile	Action	Wednesday from 7:30 to 8:30 p.m.
Buy a set of headphones for my desk so that I can stand and move while I talk on the phone	Action	Tuesday during lunch
Schedule a night out with friends by sending everyone an e-mail	Action	Monday at 6:30 a.m.
Remember to use my calm voice with the kids	Priority	As often as possible

- **Coordinate and communicate with your family, friends, coworkers, and boss as needed to make your tweaks a reality.** No one operates independently at work and in their life. That's why you want to consider whom you need to talk to and coordinate with in order to stick to your weekly *Tweak It* goals.

Most of us don't communicate with everyone we need to in order to make the flexible shifts in the way we work succeed. When asked in the 2011 Work+Life Fit Reality Check survey to rate the statement "When you make those occasional changes in how, when, and where you work, do you discuss those changes with...?" respondents replied as follows: 79 percent "your supervisor"; 63 percent "your spouse, family, or partner"; 52 percent "your colleagues"; and 45 percent "those you supervise."[2] In other words, most of us do a good job keeping our supervisors and spouses in the loop when we flex the way we work day to day, but we don't coordinate as well with our colleagues and the people we supervise. This can mean the difference between a tweak happening and not.

Here's a real-world example of why coordinating and communicating with the right people can make or break a tweak that's important to you. Because you've planned a long weekend away with your family, you will not be at work on Monday. You talk to your boss about taking the day off but fail to coordinate with your peers and the people who work for you. They're aware you're not at work, but they don't know how and when you want them to cover for you. As a result, you end up answering e-mails and returning phone calls on your day off that they could have handled. All it would have taken was a fifteen-minute conversation to tell them that you'd be out on Monday, updating them on your work and giving them permission to take over for you.

Write down how you need to coordinate and communicate for tweak success in the coming week in your *Tweak It* worksheet:

Standard Tweaks	Action or Priority	Target Date/Time	Communicate/Coordinate Plan
Pick Tweaks of the Week	Action	Sunday, 7:30 p.m.	Finish dinner and clean up without being rushed. Ask family to leave me alone for thirty minutes.
Meditate	Action	Monday–Friday, 5:30 a.m.	Set alarm for 5:15 a.m. and go to bed by 10:00 p.m.
Grocery-shop	Action	Sunday, 10:30 a.m.	Have list ready and with me so I can go right from church.
Exercise	Action	Tuesday, 6:30 a.m.; Wednesday, 5:00 p.m.; Thursday 5:00 p.m.; Friday, 6:30 a.m.; Saturday, 7:00 a.m.	Plan to arrive thirty minutes later to work on Tuesdays and Fridays; go right to the gym near work before going home on Wednesdays and Thursdays. Bring workout clothes in the car. Tell team of shift in schedule.
Connect with my husband at least once during the workday	Priority	Every morning at least	Check *Tweak It* mobile app and priority list daily as a reminder.
Find ten minutes of uninterrupted time with each of the kids	Priority	Once a day at least	Check *Tweak It* mobile app and priority list daily as a reminder.

Unique Tweaks of the Week	Action or Priority	Target Date/Time	Communicate/Coordinate Plan
Plan to do nothing	Action	Saturday, 3:00 p.m. to 5:00 p.m.	Coordinate with family and get someone else to drive kids to practice at 2:00 p.m.
Set up LinkedIn profile	Action	Wednesday, 7:30 to 8:30 p.m.	Bring my laptop home and DVR my favorite TV show that's on at 8:00 p.m.
Buy a set of head-phones for my desk so that I can stand and move while I talk on the phone	Action	Tuesday during lunch	Don't plan a lunch for Tuesday and let the rest of my team know I am not available. Allot an extra thirty minutes in case it takes longer than expected.
Schedule a night out with friends by sending everyone an e-mail	Action	Monday, 6:30 a.m.	Make sure I have everyone's e-mail address beforehand.
Remember to use my calm voice with the kids	Priority	As often as possible	Share my goal with the kids and ask for their support. Post notes around the house that say "CV" to remind me.

Track your standard and unique Tweaks of the Week progress: In addition to checking your *Tweak It* snapshot calendar and priority list regularly, you can track the progress of your tweaks during the week from your mobile device. Download your standard and unique Tweaks of the Week into the *Tweak It* app that you'll find on the *Tweak It* community website. Once a day, check in. If you see that you are off track, make adjustments and keep moving forward.

Tweak It *Phase 2—Pick Your Tweaks of the Week Summary:*

Phase 2 of the *Tweak It* practice was inspired by the final two secrets of the work+life fit naturals that I discovered in my research. The naturals continually ask themselves "What do I want in my work and life?" and when they see a mismatch between what they want and what's happening in their everyday work+life fit, they make the small choices to close the gap. The *Tweak It* practice helps you do the same thing with these three steps:

• Step 1: Review your *Tweak it* snapshot calendar and priority list from the previous week and ask, "What do I want?" This is the third secret of the work+life fit naturals. They consistently check in with themselves to understand what matters to them today.

• Step 2: Select your unique Tweaks of the Week for the next seven days. This is the fourth and final secret of the work+life fit naturals. When they see a mismatch between what's happening in their *Tweak It* snapshot and what they want, they choose small actions and priorities to close the gap.

• Step 3: Put your tweaks into your calendar and priority list, then communicate and collaborate to make them happen.

What's Next:

Periodically, in Phase 3, you'll set aside extra time to step back and do a deeper review of your longer-term goals and the *Tweak It* practice. Make the adjustments that will help you continue to build a solid foundation of well-being, satisfaction, and order. Let's take a deeper look at the steps in Phase 3—Review and Revise.

Chapter 6

Tweak It *Phase 3—Review and Revise*

You've built a solid foundation for your *Tweak It* practice in Phase 1, and you're actively picking your Tweaks of the Week so that what matters to you happens on a regular basis in Phase 2. But in Phase 3 you'll periodically, perhaps every three to six months, schedule extra time to conduct a broader review of your longer-term goals and the overall *Tweak It* practice in order to make any necessary revisions.

Your *Tweak It* Worksheet

Take a minute to visit the online community and download the *Tweak It* Worksheet. You will find a checklist that guides you through a periodic Phase 3 review.

Your longer-term goals: Sit down with your calendar and priority list. Where do you want to be next month, in the next three months, in the next year? Maybe even go as far out as the next five and ten years. To achieve those goals, what small steps do you need to take weekly as part of your Tweaks of the Week practice today? Maybe you'd like to start a business, buy a new house, or travel around the world. Input the date you want to reach that goal in your calendar, even if it's five years from now. Make note of it in the goals section of your *Tweak It* worksheet. Refer to those longer-term goals when you choose your Tweaks of the Week.

The *Tweak It* practice: How are the basics of the practice working? How might you want to revise it to become even more effective? Is the *Tweak It* snapshot calendar and priority list tracking system you're using simple and effective enough? Have you learned about a different system that you think might work better? Do you want to revise your standard tweaks? Are you measuring success the right way? Do you need to change the time and day that you pick your Tweaks of the Week?

Tweak It *Phase 3: Review and Revise Summary:*

Success with the *Tweak It* practice doesn't happen by focusing only on the week-to-week tweaks you choose but by making sure those small choices ultimately lead you to achieve both your short and long-term goals. Also, the basics of the practice need to be in good working order. Check in and revise as needed to retain effectiveness.

What's Next:

We'll look at the *Tweak It* practice in action. We'll meet Lisa, Jeff, Denise, and Pete, four people with different lives, and follow them for a four-week period as they use the three phases of the *Tweak It* practice (recapped below) to make what uniquely matters to them happen:

Phase 1: Get Started—Once and Done Steps

- Create a complete picture, or *Tweak It* snapshot, of your work+life fit today.
- Pick a simple calendar and priority list system to manage and monitor your *Tweak It* snapshot weekly.
- Decide what you want success to look like.
- Choose your standard tweaks, or small activities and priorities that will happen every week regularly.

Phase 2: Pick Your Unique Tweaks of the Week—Weekly Steps

- Review your *Tweak It* snapshot from the previous week.
- Select your unique Tweak of the Week for the next seven days.
- Put your tweaks into your calendar and priority list, then communicate and collaborate to make them happen.

Phase 3: Review Your Tweak It *Practice.* Revise—Periodic Step

How do you *Tweak It*?

Care for Yourself to Care for Others

I worked with a woman who moved to her hometown to live with her widowed father. She was a speech therapist, and she was lucky enough to land a full-time job. She was committed to making her aging father happy. This was one of those cases where she was trying to do the impossible and she nearly drove herself crazy. Then one day when she was really close to a breakdown she said, "I can't fix this, and I have to take better care of myself." She reduced her hours at work. She had been gaining weight, so she joined a health club and started exercising, lost weight, and suddenly this overwhelming task seemed much more manageable to her.

—Francine Russo, author of *They're Your Parents Too!:*
How Siblings Can Survive Their Parents' Aging
without Driving Each Other Crazy

Donations Instead of Birthday Presents

An executive in Chicago with a couple of small children changed the rules of the game related to her kids' birthday parties. Instead of presents, she had people bring pet toys, which she then donated to the animal shelter. The kids loved it. Then the other kids in the class started coming up with their own ideas of what they were going to do. It's a small act, but she took something that people don't love, such as buying a kid's birthday party gift that isn't really worth anything, and turned it around. The fact that it caught on so successfully throughout the class was a bonus.

—Sloan Berrent, founder of thecausemopolitan.com

How do you *Tweak It?*

Start a Networking Chain Reaction

This story is about a networking chain, where people, at each point, said yes to talking to someone, even though nobody knew whether it would actually lead to anything.

It started when a woman I know asked me if I would speak to her son about his career. Her son was about twenty-four. He had graduated from college and gone to Vietnam to work on a volunteer project for a year. I agreed as a favor to his mom, plus I like talking to younger people. Through the magic of modern technology, I talked to him in Vietnam on Skype. He was thinking about going to Africa, which was his real passion. As it turned out, I knew a number of people in both Vietnam and Africa. So I gave him a list of people to contact, and he followed up. He was a very good networker and he got useful information. He thanked me, and the next thing I heard, he had moved to Africa, where he had found a volunteer project to work on.

Meanwhile, I had another client who was a lawyer who had been practicing for ten years and hated his job. He had always hated it. His passion was Africa. He had no real direct experience, but he was talking to lots of people. He was also a very effective relationship builder and networker. On the off chance it might help, I said, "Maybe you should talk to this young man I just helped named Michael." I asked Michael, who was now happy in Africa, "Will you have a conversation with my lawyer client?" He said okay.

Michael and my client spoke, and it was really useful because Michael was in Africa and knew a number of little organizations that no one would be aware of here in the US. Michael's mother, the person who made the original request, reported back to me that her son had been thrilled to provide advice to my lawyer client.

My client ended up getting a job in the same nonprofit organization as Michael, as their head of administration. The organization was delighted because they would never have been able to find somebody like him on their own. Everybody, in the end, was happy with this twenty-first-century form of networking.

—Michael Melcher, author of *The Creative Lawyer: A Practical Guide to Authentic Professional Satisfaction*

How do you *Tweak It*?

Volunteer and Find Unexpected Career Success

I worked with a woman who liked her job but felt burned out. We focused on what was lacking in her life with the idea that once we identified what it was, she'd volunteer in that area. She decided that she missed being around children and wanted a volunteer job where she took care of kids. She wound up on the local school board.

She got involved and decided to run for office. She made campaign videos and learned new skills. Her professional background was technical, so she had to learn how to tell stories and be personable in a speech. She was very gung-ho, but she lost. She actually came in last out of all the serious candidates, but the benefits were huge. She became more prominent in her

(continued)

community, as well as more visible at work because people were
so interested in what she was doing. That caused her to move into
an entirely different track at work, where they are now grooming
her for senior leadership. She has already had one promotion.

—Phyllis Mufson, career coach

TWEAK IT
PRACTICE STORIES

TWEAK IT PRACTICE STORIES:

Lisa, Jeff, Denise, and Pete completed the deep dive into the three phases of *Tweak It*, and their stories will bring the practice to life. Their stories are composites of the issues, challenges, and solutions that I've heard from tens of thousands of people over my almost two decades in the work+life trenches. Chances are you'll recognize parts of your journey in their efforts to build a stronger foundation of everyday contentment, satisfaction, and order in their very different lives:

• Lisa is a global team leader at a consumer products company. She is in her midforties and has a husband, Jack, who also works full-time. They have a son, Luke, who is fourteen years old, and a daughter, Chloe, who is seven years old. After two challenging years in her business, the dust is finally settling. She wants to use the *Tweak It* practice to reconnect with her family and friends, rebuild her neglected professional network, have more fun, and take better care of herself.

- Jeff is a machinist in his early thirties who works twelve-hour shifts on rotating days. A year ago, he went through a difficult divorce and shares custody of his thirteen-year-old daughter, Ella. Having recently switched to the day shift, Jeff wants the *Tweak It* practice to help him spend quality time with his daughter, get his sleep issues under control, eat better, and work out. He'd also like to start a business on the side, try dating again, and plan the Super Bowl party that he used to love hosting every year before his divorce.

- Denise is a college administrator in her late fifties who is coping with the recent Alzheimer's diagnosis of her eighty-three-year-old father. He lives an hour away with her eighty-three-year-old mother, whose health is also frail. Denise wants the *Tweak It* practice to help coordinate with her family and set up the caregiving support both her father and mother need, while continuing to work full-time. To do this, she knows that she must also take care of herself, maintain her home, and sustain her relationship with her boyfriend, as well as not lose track of her long-term goal of finding an encore career when she retires from the college in five years.

- Pete is an entrepreneur in his late twenties who relocated a year ago from Chicago to Seattle for his wife's job. He saw the move as an opportunity to start his own business with a former colleague. During this period, he's been the go-to parent for their son, Tommy, who is turning a year old in a month. But as his business has grown, Pete's "whenever, wherever" extreme work flexibility has become a strain for him, for his business partner, and for his family. Pete wants the *Tweak It* practice to put structure around his schedule, get Tommy full-time child care, establish a regular household routine, disconnect from technology, spend more time with his wife, and, finally, get to know his new neighbors.

What makes these stories truly effective is that they utilize the tweak it advice offered by the experts I interviewed for the *Tweak It* Inspiration section of the book (chapters 11–17). You will see firsthand how their simple, get-started tips to improve your personal finances, take vacations, celebrate more, see your friends, network, and update job skills empower Lisa, Jeff, Denise, and Pete to achieve their goals. We begin by meeting Lisa.

Chapter 7

Lisa's Tweak It *Practice*

Lisa's Tweak It *Snapshot:*

Lisa is in her midforties and works for a consumer products company, where she oversees a global team of eight people. Most days she commutes forty-five minutes to her office. Her typical hours are 8:00 a.m. until 6:00 p.m., Monday through Friday; however, she has day-to-day work flexibility and typically works from home one day a week.

Because their business is global, the five brand managers on the team take turns covering international calls and meetings at night and on the weekends. That way everyone has most nights and weekends off. Lisa's night to cover is Thursday; however, she tries not to take any calls until after 8:30 p.m. so that she can spend time with her family. Periodically, Lisa needs to travel for her job, and sometimes trips are planned at the last minute if there is an issue that must be addressed immediately. Overall, Lisa tries to keep her work and life as separate as possible, working longer hours during the week, and limiting work on the weekends.

Personally, Lisa has been married to her husband, Jack, for sixteen years. They have two children: Luke, who is fourteen years old and in ninth grade, and Chloe, who is seven years old and in second grade. Jack is an engineer who works full-time for a company that is about twenty minutes from their house. He typically works from 9:00 a.m. to 5:30 p.m. at the office, which allows him to drop the kids off at school and get home to start dinner most nights. However, he often works a few hours on the weekends in order to get a jump on the coming week. As the kids get older, their needs are changing, and Lisa is aware she has to adapt how she interacts with them during the week in order to stay connected.

Phase 1: Get Started

LISA'S **TWEAK IT** *SNAPSHOT CALENDAR AND PRIORITY LIST:*

The system her company uses is Outlook. In order to keep all of her work and personal activities and priorities on the same system, Lisa is trying a color-coding system to keep track of her personal tweaks without specifying what they are. For example, weekly meal planning is a green block of time. Time with her husband, Jack, is yellow.

LISA'S DEFINITION OF **TWEAK IT** *SUCCESS:*

Because business was tough over the past two years, Lisa and her team have been working very hard and it's taken a toll on her, her friends, her family, and her extended professional relationships. Now that the dust seems to be settling and the business is recovering, Lisa wants to refocus on four areas with the *Tweak It* practice: having more fun; making more and better connections with her husband, her friends, and her children during the week; taking better care of herself; and rebuilding the professional network she's neglected over the past two years. *Tweak It* would be a success if she stopped focusing on balance but found a fit between her work and life that gave her the health, fun, and people connections she's been missing. And stopped feeling guilty about her choices.

LISA'S STANDARD TWEAKS:

When Lisa sat down to think about the small steps that were already part of her work and life, she was pleased. She wants to continue all of these activities each week:

- take thirty minutes to eat a healthy lunch, but not at her desk, and walk outside for thirty minutes three times a week
- sit down with recipes and her calendar, plan meals for the week, and make a grocery list
- have dinner together as family twice a week
- take the stairs at work instead of the elevator

Even though she's concerned she may be taking on too much, Lisa wants to add the following standard weekly tweaks to the list as well:

- pick her Tweaks of the Week on Mondays at 8:00 am when she first gets in the office

For family focus:

- turn off technology and spend thirty minutes of focused time with Jack twice a week
- ten minutes of one-on-one time with her daughter, Chloe, every day
- talk less and listen more to her son, Luke

For "me" time:

- do nothing for at least one hour twice a week
- drink more water

Phase 2: Pick Your Unique Tweaks of the Week

LISA'S TWEAKS OF THE WEEK—WEEK 1:

Lisa arrives at her desk on Monday to choose her first unique weekly tweaks. The office is quiet. She gets a cup of coffee and decides to focus her first week on putting more fun into her life. Specifically, she wants to start planning a family trip. Because of the difficulties at work, the family hasn't gone away together for an entire week in over two years.

Looking at her work commitments for the coming week, she chooses the following Tweaks of the Week and records them in her *Tweak It* worksheet along with her standard tweaks:

Lisa's Tweak It Worksheet—Week 1

Standard Tweaks	Action or Priority	Target Date/Time	Communicate/Coordinate Plan
Pick Tweaks of the Week	Action	Mon., 8 a.m.	Try not to schedule meetings until after 9 a.m.
Take thirty minutes to eat a healthy lunch but not at my desk and walk outside for thirty minutes three times a week	Action	Best days/times: Mon., 11:30 a.m.; Tues., 12:30 p.m.; and Fri., 1:00 p.m.	Shift the 1:30 p.m. meeting on Friday to 2:00 p.m.
Sit down with recipes and my calendar, plan meals for the week, and make a grocery list	Action	Sat. 2:00 p.m.	Have Jack drive Luke to soccer practice
Have dinner as a family twice a week	Action	Tues., 7:00 p.m. and Sun., 6:00 p.m.	Let everyone know those nights, and make no plans for that time
Turn off technology and spend thirty minutes of focused time with Jack twice a week	Action	Tues., 9:30 p.m. and Sat., 8:00 a.m.	Ask Jack to put times on his calendar as well
Ten minutes of one-on-one time with Chloe very day	Action	Mon.–Thurs. right before her 8:00 p.m. bedtime	No calls from overseas until after 8:30 p.m.
Talk less and listen more to Luke	Priority		Program a reminder to pop up on Outlook right before I leave work

	Action or Priority	Target Date/Time	Communicate/Coordinate Plan
Do nothing for at least one hour twice a week	Action	Sat., 3:00 p.m. and Tues., 8:30 p.m.	Have Jack pick up Luke from soccer or set up carpool. Block off the rest of Tuesday night. No calls.
Drink more water	Priority		Make sure water bottle is always full on my desk
Take the stairs at work instead of the elevator	Priority		Program a reminder in Outlook to pop up at the beginning of the workday and then again at lunch.

Unique Tweaks of the Week	Action or Priority	Target Date/Time	Communicate/Coordinate Plan
Open a travel fund and set up direct debit	Action	Thurs., 8:30 a.m., after I drop off Chloe at school	Plan to work from home on Thursday
Subscribe to travel magazines and print/cut out destination ideas	Action	Sun., 8:00 a.m.	Set the alarm to get up by 7:00 a.m.
Look at all work calendars and school schedule and pick a date for the trip	Action	Sun., 6:00 p.m., during dinner	Ask everyone to bring their schedules. Print out Luke and Chloe's school calendars.

Once Lisa's recorded her standard and unique Tweaks of the Week in her *Tweak It* worksheet, she puts them in her *Tweak It* snapshot calendar and priority list:

Lisa's Tweak It Snapshot Calendar and Priority List—Week 1

Monday	Tuesday	Wednesday	Thursday	Friday	Saturday	Sunday
Work 8:00 a.m. to 6:00 p.m. in office	Work 8:00 a.m. to 6:00 p.m. in office	Work 8:00 a.m. to 6:00 p.m. in office	Work 8:00 a.m. to 6:00 p.m. from home; overseas call/meeting coverage	Work 8:00 a.m. to 6:00 p.m. in office		
8:00 a.m.: Pick Tweaks of the Week			8:30 a.m.: Set up travel account		8:00 a.m.: Time with Jack	8:00 a.m.: Subscribe to travel info
11:30 a.m.: Lunch/Walk	12:30 p.m.: Lunch/walk			1:00 p.m.: Lunch/walk	2:00 p.m.: Recipe/meal planning 3:00 p.m.: Do nothing	
8:00 p.m.: Chloe	7:00 p.m.: Family dinner 8:00 p.m.: Chloe 8:30 p.m.: Do nothing 9:30 p.m.: Time with Jack	8:00 p.m.: Chloe	8:00 p.m.: Chloe	8:00 p.m.: Chloe		6:00 p.m.: Family dinner/Travel date planning

Priority List

✓ Take stairs at work

✓ Listen to Luke more, talk less

✓ Drink more water

LISA'S TWEAKS OF THE WEEK—WEEK 2:

Lisa starts by reviewing her progress from the previous week. Considering the last-minute overnight trip to a supplier on Tuesday, Lisa's pleased that she completed about 70 percent of the tweaks she'd planned.

Unfortunately, she missed her family time tweaks—family dinner; her tech-free, focused time with Jack; and one-on-one time with Luke and Chloe—and her thirty-minute healthy lunch and walk. But she did stick to her commitment to do nothing on Tuesday night. Instead of answering e-mails and working in the hotel, she watched a movie and it felt great.

The lesson Lisa learned from the experience is not to schedule so many family time tweaks for the same day. Spread them out. Then if something unexpected happens, it doesn't impact so many goals at once.

On the positive side, the family trip is scheduled for Spring Break in March of next year! And they all agreed to sit down together in a month and look at all the destinations they've picked from the travel resources, then choose one and book the tickets.

Turning to this week, Lisa has decided to focus her unique tweaks on her personal health and well-being. First, she wants to knit again. On the plane last week, she saw a woman knitting and remembered how much she loved it in college. Also, she wants to catch up with friends, at work and near her home, as well as spend more time on her personal appearance. The change in season from summer to fall is the perfect time to go through her closet. Once it's organized, then every night she can spend fifteen minutes before going to bed to pick out her clothes for the next day. Usually she digs something out at the last minute or wears the same outfits over and over. Not anymore.

With her tweaks and work schedule in mind, Lisa records the following activities and priorities in her *Tweak It* worksheet:

Lisa's Tweak It Worksheet—Week 2

Standard Tweaks	Action or Priority	Target Date/Time	Communicate/Coordinate Plan
Pick Tweaks of the Week	Action	Mon., 8 a.m.	Try not to schedule meetings until after 9 a.m.
Take thirty minutes to eat a healthy lunch, but not at my desk, and walk outside for thirty minutes three times a week	Action	Best days/times: Mon., 12:30 p.m.; Wed., 12:30 p.m.; and Thurs., 1:00 p.m.	Remind Susan at work that I won't shift the time blocked for lunch unless it's an emergency
Sit down with recipes and my calendar, plan meals for the week, and make grocery list	Action	Sun., 7:00 a.m.	Set my alarm to get up in time
Have dinner as family twice a week	Action	Fri., 7:00 p.m. and Sun., 6:00 p.m.	Let everyone know the nights, and make no plans for that time
Turn off technology and spend thirty minutes of focused time with Jack twice a week	Action	Wed., 9:30 p.m. and Sat., 7:30 p.m.	Ask Jack to put these times on his calendar also; see if Luke can babysit on Sat. If not, call sitter. DVR Jack's favorite show on Wednesday at 9:00 p.m.
Ten minutes of one-on-one time with Chloe every day	Action	Mon.–Fri. at 8:00 p.m.	No calls from overseas until after 8:30 p.m.
Talk less and listen more to Luke	Priority		Program a reminder to pop up on Outlook right before I leave work
Do nothing for at least one hour twice a week	Action	Sat., 3:00 p.m. and Tues., 9:00 p.m.	Have Jack pick Luke up from soccer or set up carpool
Drink more water	Priority		Make sure water bottle is always full on my desk

Unique Tweaks of the Week	Action or Priority	Target Date/Time	Communicate/Coordinate Plan
Take the stairs at work instead of the elevator	Priority		Program a reminder in Outlook to pop up at the beginning of the workday and in the middle of the day.
Visit yarn shop and buy yarn and needles	Action	Thurs., 1:00 p.m.	Forward work calls to my mobile phone so as not to miss anything important
Every time I watch TV, start to knit and expect to make mistakes	Priority		Put the knitting bag next to the couch. Ask Chloe to remind me to knit when we sit down to watch a show.
Ask Janet if she wants to go to Zumba class on Saturday morning	Action	Mon., 9:00 a.m.	Check with Jack to make sure he's fine being in charge of the kids Saturday morning
Call to catch up with Margaret, my college roommate	Action	Sun., 4:00 p.m.	Send her an e-mail earlier in the week to confirm the day/time work
Schedule lunch with Pam at work and agree not to talk business	Action	Mon., 9:00 a.m., set up; lunch Wed., 12:30 p.m.	Remind her that it will be a "work-free" conversation. Fun only.
Spend fifteen minutes the night before thinking about what's happening the next day at work and pick out my clothes	Action	Mon.–Thurs. and Sun., 10:00 p.m.	Put a note on my pillow "Pick out clothes" to remind me
Go through my closet: purge, take clothes to tailor and make list of clothes I need.	Action	Sat., 10:00 a.m.	Block off four hours on Saturday; arrange a play date for Chloe and confirm Luke's plans to limit interruptions

When Lisa's finished listing her standard and unique Tweaks of the Week in her *Tweak It* worksheet, she records them in her *Tweak It* snapshot calendar and priority list:

Lisa's Tweak It Snapshot Calendar and Priority List—Week 2

Monday	Tuesday	Wednesday	Thursday	Friday	Saturday	Sunday
Work 8:00 a.m. to 6:00 p.m. in office	Work 8:00 a.m. to 6:00 p.m. in office	Work 8:00 a.m. to 6:00 p.m. in office	Work 8:00 a.m. to 6:00 p.m. from home; overseas call/meeting coverage	Work 8:00 a.m. to 6:00 p.m. in office		
					8:00 a.m.: Zumba	7:00 a.m.: Recipes/ Meal planning
8:00 a.m.: Pick Tweaks of the Week 9:00 a.m.: E-mail Janet re. Zumba on Saturday/ Pam re. lunch on Wed. 12:30 p.m.: Lunch/walk		12:30 p.m.: Lunch with Pam	1:00 p.m.: Lunch/go to yarn store		10:00 a.m. to 2:00 p.m.: Go through closet; go to tailor/dry cleaner 3:00 p.m.: Do nothing	4:00 p.m.: Call Margaret
8:00 p.m.: Chloe 10:00 p.m.: Pick out clothes	8:00 p.m.: Chloe 9:00 p.m.: Do nothing 10:00 p.m.: Pick out clothes	8:00 p.m.: Chloe 9:30 p.m.: Time with Jack 10:00 p.m.: Pick out clothes	8:00 p.m.: Chloe 10:00 p.m.: Pick out clothes	7:00 p.m.: Family dinner 8:00 p.m.: Chloe	7:30 p.m.: Date night with Jack	6:00 p.m.: Family dinner 10:00 p.m.: Pick out clothes

Priority List

✓ Take stairs at work
✓ Listen to Luke more, talk less
✓ Drink more water
✓ Every time watch TV, knit

LISA'S TWEAKS OF THE WEEK—WEEK 3:

Again, Lisa didn't complete all of the tweaks she'd planned. Last week, two members of her team were sick, which meant she had to provide overseas call and meeting coverage on Tuesday, Wednesday, and Thursday. Thankfully, Tuesday night was quiet, but on Wednesday, she was on either the phone or a video conference call from 7:30 to 10:30 p.m. Again, she missed one of her tech-free focus times with Jack and one-on-one time with Chloe. And she was too tired to pick out her clothes before bed. Then, a meeting ran long on Wednesday and caused her to miss her lunch with Pam.

The good news is that she did start to knit, although she realized that she doesn't watch enough television to make that the only time she practices. So she is going to knit during Luke's soccer games as well. She went through her closet and picked out her clothes every other night of the week. She felt much more put together and calm when she left for work. In fact, she's making both the knitting and evening clothes selection two of her standard tweaks.

The lesson learned for the week was, you don't have to achieve every tweak to see a noticeable difference in what you are able to accomplish. Four nights of one-on-one time with Chloe is better than none. This week Lisa turns her attention to getting the kids organized. With the kids in two different schools, she's learned that getting set up at the beginning of the year makes everything run much more smoothly. Last year she didn't do it and everyone suffered. Not this year. She lists the following Tweaks of the Week in her *Tweak It* worksheet:

Lisa's Tweak It Worksheet—Week 3

Standard Tweaks	Action or Priority	Target Date/Time	Communicate/Coordinate Plan
Pick Tweaks of the Week	Action	Mon., 8:00 a.m.	Try not to schedule meetings until after 9:00 a.m.
Take thirty minutes to eat a healthy lunch, but not at my desk, and walk outside for thirty minutes three times a week	Action	Best days/times: Mon., 12:00 p.m.; Thurs., 12:30 p.m.; Fri., 11:30 a.m.	
Sit down with recipes and my calendar, plan meals for the week, and make grocery list	Action	Sun., 4:00 p.m.	Put the recipes on the counter before we leave for our weekend trip
Have dinner as family twice a week	Action	Sun., 7:00 p.m.; Wed. 6:30 p.m.	Let everyone know the nights, and make no plans for that time
Turn off technology and spend thirty minutes of focused time with Jack twice a week	Action	Tues., 9:30 p.m.; Sat., 7:00 a.m.	Switched back to Tuesday; ask Jack to put these times on his calendar also
Ten minutes of one-on-one time with Chloe every day	Action	Mon.–Fri. at 8:00 p.m.	No calls from overseas until after 8:30 p.m.
Talk less and listen more to Luke	Priority		Program a reminder to pop up on Outlook right before I leave work
Do nothing for at least one hour twice a week	Action	Fri, 9:00 p.m.; no slot this week for 2nd time	Make sure everyone has plans and rides so the time isn't interrupted
Drink more water	Priority		Make sure water bottle is always full on my desk
Take the stairs at work instead of the elevator	Priority		Program a reminder in Outlook to pop up at the beginning of the workday and in the middle of the day

Unique Tweaks of the Week	Action or Priority	Target Date/Time	Communicate/Coordinate Plan
Knit when watching TV and at Luke's soccer games	Priority		Put knitting bag near couch and bring it in the car
Pick out clothes for next workday	Action	Mon.–Thurs. and Sun. at 10:00 p.m.	
Go to elementary school website and bookmark Facebook and teacher pages	Action	Mon., 3:00 p.m.	Look up site URL in the directory before work
Go to high school website and bookmark Facebook and teacher pages	Action	Mon., 3:00 p.m.	Look up site URL in the directory before work
Put important school dates in my calendar	Action	Tues., 10:00 a.m.	
Sign up for alerts and e-mails from the schools	Action	Wed., 2:00 p.m.	Have alerts sent to both me and Jack
Send introduction e-mail to Chloe's elementary school teacher	Action	Thurs., 11:00 a.m.	Copy Jack on the e-mail to introduce him as well
Send introduction e-mail to Luke's history and English teachers because you know those are the classes he'll struggle with	Action	Fri., 2:00 p.m.	Confirm the teachers to be contacted with Luke; copy Jack on e-mail to introduce him as well
Sign up to have both you and Luke get the College Board's Question of the Day e-mail and discuss	Action	Sat., 8:00 a.m.	Answer the first question with Luke in the car when we go away this weekend
Review progress with college savings with Jack	Action	Sun., 8:00 p.m.	Put the file with the statements on the counter before we leave for the weekend

Once Lisa's recorded her standard and unique Tweaks of the Week in her *Tweak It* worksheet, she puts them in her *Tweak It* snapshot calendar and priority list:

Lisa's Tweak It Snapshot Calendar and Priority List—Week 3

Monday	Tuesday	Wednesday	Thursday	Friday	Saturday	Sunday
Work 8:00 a.m. to 7:00 p.m. in office (Late meeting at work)	Work 8:00 a.m. to 6:00 p.m. in office	Work 8:00 a.m. to 6:00 p.m. from home	Work 8:00 a.m. to 6:00 p.m. in office with overseas call/meeting coverage	Work 8:00 a.m. to 6:00 p.m. in office		
					7:00 a.m.: Time with Jack 8:00 a.m.: Sign me and Luke up for College Board Question of Day e-mail	AWAY FOR WEEKEND
8:00 a.m.: Pick Tweaks of the Week 3:00 p.m.: Bookmark elementary/high school sites	10:00 a.m.: Put important school dates into calendar 12:00 p.m.: Lunch/walk	2:00 p.m.: Sign up for alerts from schools	11:00 a.m.: Send introduction e-mail to Chloe's teacher 12:30 p.m.: Lunch/walk	11:30 a.m.: Lunch/walk 2:00 p.m.: Send introduction e-mails to Luke's teachers	AWAY FOR WEEKEND	4:00 p.m.: Recipes/Meal planning
10:00 p.m.: Pick out clothes	8:00 p.m.: Chloe 9:30 p.m.: Time with Jack 10:00 p.m.: Pick out clothes	6:30 p.m.: Family dinner 8:00 p.m.: Chloe 10:00 p.m.: Pick out clothes	8:00 p.m.: Chloe 10:00 p.m.: Pick out clothes	8:00 p.m.: Chloe 9:00 p.m.: Do nothing		7:00 p.m.: Family dinner 8:00 p.m.: Review college savings 10:00 p.m.: Pick out clothes

Priority List

✓ Take stairs at work
✓ Listen to Luke more, talk less
✓ Drink more water
✓ Every time watch TV, knit
✓ Pick out clothes the night before

LISA'S TWEAKS OF THE WEEK—WEEK 4:

Lisa lost a lot of time over the weekend that she usually uses to get things done because they visited friends overnight. Regardless, she accomplished almost all of her tweaks for the week. And everyone had a wonderful time with their friends and vowed to do it again soon. She didn't get a chance to sign up for the Question of the Day from the College Board. She'll put that back on her list in a month or so. Since Luke is only starting ninth grade it isn't urgent, but friends who follow a blog called the Perfect Score Project (www.perfectscoreproject.com) have told her it does help prepare for the test.

Next week at work is going to be tough because a big project is due on Thursday, which will mean at least one late night and an early morning. But Lisa doesn't want to ignore her professional network any longer. She wants to set up a way to track a deliberate, ongoing outreach to business contacts, new and old. And she'd finally like to fill out her profile on LinkedIn and begin to join conversations in at least two industry groups.

Planning accordingly, she records the following Tweaks of the Week in her *Tweak It* worksheet:

Lisa's Tweak It Worksheet—Week 4

Standard Tweaks	Action or Priority	Target Date/Time	Communicate/Coordinate Plan
Pick Tweaks of the Week	Action	Mon., 8:00 a.m.	Try not to schedule meetings until after 9:00 a.m.
Take thirty minutes to eat a healthy lunch, but not at my desk, and walk outside for thirty minutes three times a week	Action	Best date/time: Fri., 1:00 p.m.	No other time this week because of the project, and I don't want to overcommit. The project is due Thursday; therefore, lunch is realistic on Friday when I work from home.
Sit down with recipes and my calendar, plan meals for the week, and make grocery list	Action	Sun., 8:00 a.m.	Put recipes and calendar on the counter before I go to bed
Have dinner as family twice a week	Action	Mon., 7:00 p.m.; Sat., 6:00 p.m.	Let everyone know the nights, and make no plans for that time
Turn off technology and spend thirty minutes of focused time with Jack twice a week	Action	Sat., 8 p.m.	Ask Jack to put this time on his calendar also; no other option to spend focus time together because of project
Ten minutes of one-on-one time with Chloe every day	Action	Mon., Tues., Thurs., 8:00 p.m.	No calls from overseas until after 8:30 p.m.
Talk less and listen more to Luke	Priority		Program a reminder to pop up on Outlook right before I leave work
Do nothing for at least one hour this week (two times not going to work because of schedule)	Action	Fri., 8 p.m.	Confirm everyone's plan for the evening in advance

Unique Tweaks of the Week	Action or Priority	Target Date/Time	Communicate/Coordinate Plan
Drink more water	Priority		Make sure water bottle is always full on my desk
Take the stairs at work instead of the elevator	Priority		Program a reminder in Outlook to pop up at the beginning of the workday and in the middle of the day
Set up a log in Excel to plan and track who I call or e-mail to network	Action	Mon., 2:00 p.m.	Remind your team you have a 1:45 p.m. "hard stop" for the 1:00 p.m. meeting
Introduce two people I know who share interests and could help each other	Action	Tues., 8:30 a.m.	Give some thought to the two people to connect beforehand
Research jobs in my field and at the level I want to advance to. Write down the common keywords to use when I set up online profile.	Action	Fri., 5:00 p.m.	Working from home on Friday. Make sure meetings done by 5:00 p.m. and switch focus to job keyword research.
Set up a LinkedIn profile and write biography using keywords I found	Action	Sat., 8:00 a.m.	Ask family to give you a couple of hours of uninterrupted time to focus
Ask for and give LinkedIn recommendations to three people	Action	Sat., 8:00 a.m.	Think about to whom you should ask, and offer to write a recommendation for them
Join a couple of industry groups on LinkedIn and follow the conversation	Action	Sun., 8:00 p.m.	Block off an hour to spend time looking at groups and listening to their conversations
Answer two questions posted in the LinkedIn groups	Action	Sun., 8:00 p.m.	

When Lisa's finished listing her standard and unique Tweaks of the Week in her *Tweak It* worksheet, she records them in her *Tweak It* snapshot calendar and priority list:

Lisa's Tweak It Snapshot Calendar and Priority List—Week 4

Monday	Tuesday	Wednesday	Thursday	Friday	Saturday	Sunday
Work 7:00 a.m. to 5:00 p.m. in office (Go to work early/come home earlier)	Work 8:00 a.m. to 6:00 p.m. in office	Work 8:00 a.m. to 9:00 p.m. in office (home late)	Work 8:00 a.m. to 6:00 p.m. in office Go to work early; with overseas call/meeting coverage	Work 8:00 a.m. to 6:00 p.m. from home		
		7:00 a.m.: Chloe			8:00 a.m.: Set up LinkedIn profile and write bio/ ask for and give recs	8:00 a.m.: Recipe/meal planning
8:00 a.m.: Pick Tweaks of the Week 2:00 p.m.: Set up Excel spreadsheet to track networking	8:30 a.m.: Introduce two people via e-mail			1:00 p.m.: Lunch/walk 5:00 p.m.: Research jobs for keywords		4:00 p.m.: Luke soccer game
7:00 p.m.: Family dinner 8:00 p.m.: Chloe 10:30 p.m.: Pick out clothes	8:00 p.m.: Chloe	10:00 p.m.: Pick out clothes	8:00 p.m.: Chloe 10:00 p.m.: Pick out clothes	8:00 p.m.: Do nothing	6:00 p.m.: Family dinner 8:00 p.m.: Time with Jack	8:00 p.m.: Join two LinkedIn groups and answer one question 10:00 p.m.: Pick out clothes

Priority List

✓ Take stairs at work
✓ Listen to Luke more, talk less
✓ Drink more water
✓ Every time watch TV, knit
✓ Pick out clothes the night before

Phase 3: Review and Revise

When Lisa sat down to review where she was after four weeks of working with the *Tweak It* practice, she felt she'd started to achieve her goals. She was having more fun, connecting more often and more deeply with her family and friends, feeling better about her personal appearance, and establishing strong relationships with the kids' schools. There were a couple of aspects of the practice that she wanted to "tweak," such as:

TWEAK IT *SNAPSHOT CALENDAR AND PRIORITY LIST:*

Happily, there are too many tweaks for her to keep track of through color coding. Therefore, she's going to start tracking her personal activities and priorities on a Google Calendar that she'll have open during the day and refer to often.

TWEAK IT *SUCCESS:*

A perfectionist by nature, Lisa is trying to celebrate when she achieves 70 percent of her tweaks for a given week. And by focusing on the actions and priorities that give her the highest time and energy return, like time with her family and friends, taking care of herself, and strengthening her professional network, she feels so much better.

STANDARD TWEAKS:

Now that Luke's in high school, he is twice as busy. So she needs to work with him to find more structured opportunities for them to connect and spend time together.

Chapter 8

Jeff's Tweak It *Practice*

Jeff's Tweak It *Snapshot:*

Jeff, in his early thirties, is a machinist who has worked at the same plant thirty minutes from his house for the past ten years. He recently switched from the night shift and will work the day shift for the next six months. Although his hours are set at 6 a.m. to 6 p.m., the days he works will rotate each week. He has little day-to-day flexibility in his hours and periodically must work mandatory overtime. Because some weeks he will have five days off, he's thinking of starting a handyman business on the side, doing small projects for neighbors to make extra money.

Jeff and his ex-wife went through a difficult divorce a year ago, and they now share custody of thirteen-year-old Ella, who spends at least two nights a week with Jeff. Now that he's working the day shift, he wants to get a number of areas in his life back on track. This includes dealing with his chronic sleep issues, his lack of exercise, and some unhealthy eating habits. Although he's a little hesitant, he wants to try to reenter the dating scene and even hold his annual Super Bowl party for the first time in two years.

Phase 1: Get Started

JEFF'S **TWEAK IT** *SNAPSHOT CALENDAR AND PRIORITY LIST:*

When his rotation schedule is set for the month, he inputs it into a Google Calendar that he then shares with his ex-wife. He then keeps all of his personal activities and priorities in a separate Google Calendar that only he sees. He can display the Google work and personal calendars at the same time.

JEFF'S DEFINITION OF **TWEAK IT** *SUCCESS:*

For Jeff, *Tweak It* will be a success if he sees concrete improvement in these areas: (1) he can get to sleep and is sleeping through the night, (2) he feels better physically, (3) he is spending regular quality time with his daughter, (4) he has started his handyman business, and (5) he has gotten a date.

JEFF'S STANDARD TWEAKS:

Because of his unpredictable schedule, Jeff chooses the first day he doesn't work in a given week to pick his Tweaks of the Week. Some weeks that will be Monday, and other weeks it will be Wednesday.

Jeff also wants to continue to write in his journal, a practice he started during his divorce to deal with the stress of the experience. He found it surprisingly helpful. Another routine he enjoys is connecting with his daughter either by phone, text, or e-mail twice a day. It's a great way to remain active in her life even though he doesn't see her all the time.

The new standard tweaks he wants to add are health and sleep related. Since he has a job with an irregular schedule, Jeff is convinced the only way to stay healthy is by establishing some sort of a routine. Over the last year, he let that slide. Jeff's been advised that if he wants to improve his sleep he should go to bed and get up at the same time every day. So, Jeff will try to go to bed at 10 p.m. on the nights before a workday and get up at 5 a.m. in order to be to work when his shift starts at 6 a.m. On non-workdays, he'll go to bed and get up one hour later in order to keep his sleep routine as consistent as possible. The next standard tweak is to do cardio exercise at the gym two to three times a week. Finally, eat two healthy meals a day.

Phase 2: Pick Your Unique Tweaks of the Week

JEFF'S TWEAKS OF THE WEEK—WEEK 1

Jeff decided to tackle one or two steps toward all of his goals each week rather than take one goal on at a time. He's going to start to meet people by joining the town coed softball league. His neighbor plays, enjoys it, and assures him that it's a low-key and flexible commitment. Then he's going to let people know about the Super Bowl party at the end of the month. Next he'll turn his attention to learning about what it means to run a business and get a handle on his finances.

In terms of his health, he needs to find a doctor and buy and install blackout shades in his bedroom to help him sleep. Last but not least there's Ella. They love to go on daylong adventures together, and in the winter that includes skiing. He wants to start planning a trip to a slope that they've never skied before. Finally, he thinks it's time to sit down and talk to Ella about the rules for using her cell phone and the Internet. His niece had a bad experience and he wants Ella to avoid the same mistakes.

Jeff's Tweak It Worksheet—Week 1

Standard Tweaks	Action or Priority	Target Date/Time	Communicate/Coordinate Plan
Pick Tweaks of the Week	Action	Wed., 8:00 a.m.	Leave extra time after I journal the first time each week
Write in journal twice	Action	Wed., 8:00 a.m.; Thurs., 8:00 a.m.	Put journal out on the counter as a reminder
Connect with daughter daily by phone, text, or e-mail	Priority		Set reminder on cell phone
Cardio at the gym twice a week	Action	Wed., 10:00 a.m.; Thurs., 10:00 a.m.	Leave gym clothes out the night before
Eat two healthy meals a day	Action	Workdays: lunch and dinner; off days: breakfast and dinner	Premake simple meals for dinner and try to plan what I'm going to eat for lunch the night before
Go to bed and get up at same time each day	Action	5:00 a.m. wake up; 10:00 p.m. to bed on workdays; one hour later on non-workdays	Make plans that allow me to get ready and in bed by 10:00 p.m., especially on worknights when I need to be up by 5:00 a.m. the next day

Unique Tweaks of the Week	Action or Priority	Target Date/Time	Communicate/Coordinate Plan
Sign up for town coed softball league	Action	Wed., 12:00 p.m.	Go right from gym to sign up at the town community center
Decide who to invite to Super Bowl party and send an electronic invitation	Action	Mon., 7:30 p.m.	Do that before I turn on the TV
Reach out to two entrepreneurs I know to learn about their experience	Action	Thurs., 12:00 p.m.	Do research on their businesses beforehand to mention something I admire in the e-mail
Calculate monthly earnings and expenses	Action	Thurs., 4:00 p.m.	Find calculator
Ask friends to recommend a local doctor	Action	Fri., 7:30 p.m.	
Buy and install blackout shades for the bedroom	Action	Wed., 2:00 p.m.	Measure windows before I go to the gym
Research local ski slopes for my trip with Ella	Action	Wed., 7:30 p.m.	
Download cell phone and Internet online rules contract* for Ella	Action	Sat., 8:00 p.m.	

*An example of a contract is available at www.shawnedgington.com/essential-parent-resource-kit/.

When Jeff finished listing his standard and unique Tweaks of the Week in his *Tweak It* worksheet, he recorded them in his *Tweak It* snapshot calendar and priority list:

Jeff's Tweak It Snapshot Calendar and Priority List—Week 1

Monday	Tuesday	Wednesday	Thursday	Friday	Saturday	Sunday
Work 6:00 a.m. to 6:00 p.m.	Work 6:00 a.m. to 6:00 p.m.	OFF	OFF	Work 6:00 a.m. to 6:00 p.m.	Work 6:00 a.m. to 6:00 p.m.	Work 6:00 a.m. to 6:00 p.m.
		7:00 a.m.: Breakfast and take Ella to school 8:00 a.m.: Write in journal/ Pick Tweaks of the Week	7:00 a.m.: Breakfast and take Ella to school 8:00 a.m.: Write in journal			
12:00 p.m.: Lunch (packed at home)	12:00 p.m.: Lunch (packed at home)	10:00 a.m.: Gym 12:00 p.m.: Register for softball 2:00 p.m.: Buy and install blackout shades in bedroom 4:00 p.m.: Pick up Ella after school	10:00 a.m.: Gym 12:00 p.m.: Send e-mails to two entrepreneurs to ask about business 4:00 p.m.: Calculate monthly income and expenses	12:00 p.m.: Lunch (packed at home)	12:00 p.m.: Lunch (packed at home)	12:00 p.m.: Lunch (packed at home)
7:00 p.m.: Dinner and pack lunch 7:30 p.m.: Create an invite list for Super Bowl Party and send e-vite 10:00 p.m.: To bed	6:30 p.m.: Pick up Ella for dinner and sleepover 7:00 p.m.: Dinner and pack lunch 10:00 p.m.: To bed	6:00 p.m.: Dinner with Ella 7:30 p.m.: Research hours and trails of local ski resort 10:00 p.m.: To bed	7:00 p.m.: Dinner and pack lunch 10:00 p.m.: To bed	7:00 p.m.: Dinner and pack lunch 7:30 p.m.: Call three local friends for doctor suggestions 10:00 p.m.: To bed	7:00 p.m.: Dinner and pack lunch 8:00 p.m.: Download online/cell phone contract for Ella to sign 10:00 p.m.: To bed	6:30 p.m.: Pick up Ella for dinner and to stay over 11:00 p.m.: To bed

Priority List

✓ Connect with Ella either by phone, text, or e-mail twice a day

JEFF'S TWEAKS OF THE WEEK—WEEK 2

Last week, Jeff worked five days, three of which were Friday, Saturday, and Sunday. This made seeing Ella more difficult. To make up for it, he'd planned to pick her up to sleep over on Tuesday after work. Unfortunately, he had to work mandatory overtime that night, and by the time he was ready to leave it was too late. Because of the mandatory overtime, he couldn't get doctor references, but he ended up doing it during his breaks at work on Saturday instead. He learned that he needs to talk to his floor manager to see if he could be scheduled for mandatory overtime on the nights he doesn't have Ella. Otherwise, Jeff accomplished all of the other tweaks he had planned, and the blackout shades were already making a difference in his sleep.

This week is more of the same: continue to take small steps to reach his main goals of better health and better sleep, connect with his daughter, start his business, set up an emergency fund, get a physical, plan the party, and perhaps get a date.

Jeff's Tweak It Worksheet—Week 2

Standard Tweaks	Action or Priority	Target Date/Time	Communicate/Coordinate Plan
Pick Tweaks of the Week	Action	Wed., 8:00 a.m.	Leave extra time after I journal the first time each week
Write in journal two or three times	Action	Mon., Tues., and Sun., 8:00 a.m.	Put journal out on the counter as a reminder
Connect with daughter daily by phone, text, or e-mail	Priority		Set reminder on cell phone
Cardio at the gym three times a week	Action	Mon., Tues., and Sun., 10:00 a.m.	Leave gym clothes out the night before
Eat two healthy meals a day	Action	Workdays: lunch and dinner; off days: breakfast and dinner	Premake simple meals for dinner and try to plan what I'm going to eat for lunch the night before
Go to bed and get up a same time each day	Action	5:00 a.m., wake up; 10:00 p.m., to bed on work days; one hour later on non-workdays	Make plans that allow me to get ready and in bed by 10:00 p.m. especially on work-nights when I need to be up by 5:00 a.m. the next day

Unique Tweaks of the Week	Action or Priority	Target Date/Time	Communicate/Coordinate Plan
Create list of things I need for the Super Bowl party	Action	Tues., 12:00 p.m.	Look at book *Plan to Party* for to-do checklists for party
Eat lunch with Cynthia and Janice at work and ask them if they have friends I might want to ask out on a date	Action	Wed., 12:00 p.m.	
Plan time to talk to Ella and have her sign the phone/online contract	Action	Mon., 6:00 p.m.	Give Ella heads-up that this is the topic of our conversation
Meet with entrepreneurs, and find two businesses I admire and study their business model	Action	Sun., 12:00 p.m.: meet; Sun. 3:00 p.m.: study	Block off the afternoon
Open an online emergency savings account and set up direct debit	Action	Fri., 10:00 a.m.	
Check insurance to see which recommended doctors are in my plan	Action	Fri., 12:00 p.m.	
Buy and install dimmers for the lights in the house and lower lights two hours before bed	Action	Mon., 12:00 p.m.	Count number of switches before I leave for the gym
Show Ella information about the ski slope	Action	Fri., 6:00 p.m.	

Once Jeff's recorded his standard and unique Tweaks of the Week in his *Tweak It* worksheet, he puts them in his calendar and priority list:

Jeff's Tweak It Calendar and Priority List—Week 2

Monday	Tuesday	Wednesday	Thursday	Friday	Saturday	Sunday
OFF	OFF	Work 6:00 a.m. to 6:00 p.m.	Work 6:00 a.m. to 6:00 p.m.	OFF	OFF	OFF
7:00 a.m.: Breakfast and take Ella to school 8:00 a.m.: Write in journal/ Pick Tweaks of the Week	7:00 a.m.: Breakfast and take Ella to school 8:00 a.m.: Write in journal			8:00 a.m.: Write in journal	9:00 a.m.: Breakfast with Ella	8:00 a.m.: Write in journal
10:00 a.m.: Gym 12:00 p.m.: Buy and install dimmers 4:00 p.m.: Pick up Ella after school	10:00 a.m.: Gym 12:00 p.m.: Create list of items to buy for Super Bowl party	12:00 p.m.: Lunch (packed at home); eat with Cynthia and Janice to ask about friends	12:00 p.m.: Lunch (packed at home)	10:00 a.m.: Open online emergency fund account 12:00 p.m.: Confirm recommended doctors in network 4:00 p.m.: Pick up Ella after school	4:00 p.m.: Drive Ella home	10:00 a.m.: Gym 12:00 p.m.: Meet with two entrepreneurs 3:00 p.m.: Find two businesses online to study
6:00 p.m.: Dinner with Ella; talk about online/cell phone contract 9:00 p.m.: Dim lights before bed 11:00 p.m.: To bed	6:00 p.m.: Dinner and pack lunch 8:00 p.m.: Dim lights before bed 10:00 p.m.: To bed	7:00 p.m.: Dinner and pack lunch 8:00 p.m.: Dim lights before bed 10:00 p.m.: To bed	7:00 p.m.: Dinner 9:00 p.m.: Dim lights before bed 11:00 p.m.: To bed	6:00 p.m.: Dinner with Ella; show her information about the local ski slope 9:00 p.m.: Dim lights before bed 11:00 p.m.: To bed	6:00 p.m.: Dinner with friends 9:00 p.m.: Dim lights before bed 11:00 p.m.: To bed	7:00 p.m.: Dinner and pack lunch 8:00 p.m.: Dim lights before bed 10:00 p.m.: To bed

Priority List

✓ Connect with Ella either by phone, text, or e-mail twice a day

JEFF'S TWEAKS OF THE WEEK—WEEK 3

Not surprisingly, having five days off in the week helped Jeff accomplish all of the tweaks he had planned. He found he had plenty of time left over that he could easily devote to his handyman business. Next week he's back to working five days, three of which are over the weekend. But he has momentum and is optimistic he can continue the progress he's making.

The party preparation and ski trip planning are going well, as are his conversations with Ella about her phone and Facebook use. He plans to sign up for the newsletters and Facebook pages of the two businesses he's been studying. Sleep is still an issue even with the blackout shades and dimmers. He's going to follow the advice he heard recently from Ben Rubin, the cofounder of a sleep solutions company called Zeo. Rubin suggested buying a pair of blue-blocking (orange) glasses and putting them on two hours before bed to reset his internal body clock. Jeff's willing to give it a try. To meet people, Jeff will make it a priority to be more open to women who make an effort to be friendly with him at the gym. You never know. Finally, he's planning to review his 401(k) and organize the equipment for his trip with Ella.

Jeff's Tweak It Worksheet—Week 3

Standard Tweaks	Action or Priority	Target Date/Time	Communicate/Coordinate Plan
Pick Tweaks of the Week	Action	Wed., 8:00 a.m.	Leave extra time after I journal the first time each week
Write in journal twice	Action	Wed. and Thurs., 8:00 a.m.	Put journal out on the counter as a reminder
Connect with daughter daily by phone, text, or e-mail	Priority		Set reminder on cell phone
Cardio at the gym two times a week	Action	Wed. and Thurs., 10:00 a.m.	Leave gym clothes out the night before
Eat two healthy meals a day	Action	Workdays: lunch and dinner; off days: breakfast and dinner	Premake simple meals for dinner and try to plan what I'm going to eat for lunch the night before
Go to bed and get up at same time each day	Action	5:00 a.m. wake up; 10:00 p.m. to bed on workdays; one hour later on non-workdays	Make plans that allow me to get ready and in bed by 10:00 p.m., especially on work-nights when I need to be up by 5:00 a.m. the next day

Unique Tweaks of the Week	Action or Priority	Target Date/Time	Communicate/Coordinate Plan
Shop for the Super Bowl party	Action	Wed., 12:00 p.m.	Bring the list to the gym
Do a Google search of Ella's name to see what sites come up	Action	Tues., 8:15 p.m.	
Get newsletters and follow on Facebook the two companies I am studying	Action	Mon., 8:15 p.m.	
Review my 401(k) account and deposit amount	Action	Fri., 8:15 p.m.	Make sure I have login information. If not, get it from HR at work.
Stop and check out offices of three doctors recommended	Action	Thurs., 12:00 p.m.	Bring names and addresses of doctors to the gym
Buy blue-blocking glasses and put them on two hours before bed	Action	Wed., 2:00 p.m.	Do web search to find where glasses are sold
Organize equipment for ski trip with Ella	Action	Sat., 8:15 p.m.	Ask Ella to bring her equipment with her on Wednesday when I pick her up

When Jeff finished listing his standard and unique Tweaks of the Week in his *Tweak It* worksheet, he recorded them in his *Tweak It* snapshot calendar and priority list:

Jeff's Tweak It Snapshot Calendar and Priority List—Week 3

Monday	Tuesday	Wednesday	Thursday	Friday	Saturday	Sunday
Work 6:00 a.m. to 6:00 p.m.	Work 6:00 a.m. to 6:00 p.m.	OFF	OFF	Work 6:00 a.m. to 6:00 p.m.	Work 6:00 a.m. to 6:00 p.m.	Work 6:00 a.m. to 6:00 p.m.
		7:00 a.m.: Breakfast and take Ella to school 8:00 a.m.: Write in journal/ Pick Tweaks of the Week	7:00 a.m.: Breakfast and take Ella to school 8:00 a.m.: Write in journal			
12:00 p.m.: Lunch (packed at home)	12:00 p.m.: Lunch (packed at home)	10:00 a.m.: Gym 12:00 p.m.: Shop for Super Bowl party 2:00 p.m.: Buy blue-blocking glasses 4:00 p.m.: Pick up Ella after school	10:00 a.m.: Gym 12:00 p.m.: Check out offices of three doctors recommended	12:00 p.m.: Lunch (packed at home)	12:00 p.m.: Lunch (packed at home)	12:00 p.m.: Lunch (packed at home)
7:00 p.m.: Dinner and pack lunch 8:00 p.m.: Dim lights before bed 8:15 p.m.: Sign up to follow and get newsletters of two model companies 10:00 p.m.: To bed	7:00 p.m.: Dinner and pack lunch 6:30 p.m.: Pick up Ella for dinner and sleepover 8:15 p.m.: Do a Google search with Ella's name 9:00 p.m.: Dim lights before bed 11:00 p.m.: To bed	6:00 p.m.: Dinner with Ella 9:00 p.m.: Dim lights and put on glasses before bed 11:00 p.m.: To bed	6:00 p.m.: Dinner and pack lunch 8:00 p.m.: Dim lights and put on glasses before bed 10:00 p.m.: To bed	7:00 p.m.: Dinner and pack lunch 8:00 p.m.: Dim lights and put on glasses before bed 8:15 p.m.: Review 401(k) account 10:00 p.m.: To bed	7:00 p.m.: Dinner and pack lunch 8:00 p.m.: Dim lights and put on glasses before bed 8:15 p.m.: Organize ski equipment for trip with Ella 10:00 p.m.: To bed	7:00 p.m.: Dinner and pack lunch 6:30 p.m.: Pick up Ella for dinner and sleepover 9:00 p.m.: Dim lights and put on glasses before bed 11:00 p.m.: To bed

Priority List

✓ Connect with Ella either by phone, text, or e-mail twice a day

✓ Be more aware when I'm at the gym of women who make an effort to connect

JEFF'S TWEAKS OF THE WEEK—WEEK 4

It's becoming clear that it is more difficult for Jeff to accomplish all of his tweaks during the weeks that he works twelve hours a day five days a week. He would have completed almost every activity and priority he had planned, but he hurt his hand at work on Tuesday. While the injury wasn't severe, the doctor at the clinic suggested he rest his hand during his Tuesday and Wednesday days off. As a result, he couldn't go to the gym or shop for the Super Bowl party as he had hoped. Thankfully, his hand is on the mend and he can make up for lost time this week. He's even going to take the risk and invite Leslie, a friend of his friend Cynthia's, to the Super Bowl party on Sunday.

Regarding his handyman business, he feels that he has enough information to move ahead. While the Google search under Ella's name revealed the Facebook page she'd told him about, now he wants to be able to sign on to Facebook using her login and monitor it. He's looking forward to skiing with Ella Saturday, and he wants to set up a 529 college savings account for her this week. His goal is to put most of the money from his handyman business into the account.

Sleep is the final challenge. While it is much better with the blackout shades, the dimmers, and the blue-blocking glasses, Jeff heard the problem might be bright light from his computer monitor. To address this, Jeff is going to install a program on his computer that regulates the amount of light on the screen.

Jeff's Tweak It Worksheet—Week 4

Standard Tweaks	Action or Priority	Target Date/Time	Communicate/Coordinate Plan
Pick Tweaks of the Week	Action	Wed, 8:00 a.m.	Leave extra time after I journal the first time each week
Write in journal four times	Action	Mon., Tues., Fri., Sun., at 8:00 a.m.	Put journal out on the counter as a reminder
Connect with daughter daily by phone, text, or e-mail	Priority		Set reminder on cell phone
Cardio at the gym four times	Action	Mon., Tues., Fri., Sun., at 10:00 a.m.	Leave gym clothes out the night before
Eat two healthy meals a day	Action	Workdays: lunch and dinner; off days: breakfast and dinner	Premake simple meals for dinner and try to plan what I'm going to eat for lunch the night before
Go to bed and get up at same time each day	Action	5:00 a.m. wake up; 10:00 p.m. to bed on workdays; one hour later on non-workdays	Make plans that allow me to get ready and in bed by 10:00 p.m., especially on work-nights when I need to be up by 5:00 a.m. the next day

Unique Tweaks of the Week	Action or Priority	Target Date/Time	Communicate/Coordinate Plan
Shop for Super Bowl party; clean the apartment and prepare food	Action	Tues, 12:00 p.m.	Bring the list to the gym and block off the entire afternoon
Host Super Bowl party	Action	Sun., 5:00 p.m.	Have everything ready by 3:00 p.m. so that I have two hours to relax beforehand
Ask Cynthia's friend, Leslie, to Super Bowl party	Action	Wed., 8:15 p.m.	Get her contact information from Cynthia at work
Get Ella's passwords and login in and review her sites	Action	Fri, 8:15 p.m.	
Register company LLC and get URL for site	Action	Fri, 12:00 p.m.	Finalize the company name and register URL
Open 529 account for Ella's education	Action	Mon., 12:00 p.m.	Get her birth certificate from my ex-wife after I drop Ella at school
Schedule a physical with the doctor I liked best	Action	Mon., 2:00 p.m.	Ask when I need to get the blood work taken
Install program on my computer that automatically reduces the light from the monitor*	Action	Thurs. 8:00 p.m.	
Ski with Ella	Action	Sat. 9:00 a.m.	

* An example of a light-reduction program is f.lux; see www.stereopsis.com/flux/

Once Jeff's recorded his standard and unique Tweaks of the Week in his *Tweak It* worksheet, he puts them in his *Tweak It* snapshot calendar and priority list:

Jeff's Tweak It Snapshot Calendar and Priority List—Week 4

Monday	Tuesday	Wednesday	Thursday	Friday	Saturday	Sunday
OFF	OFF	Work 6:00 a.m. to 6:00 p.m.	Work 6:00 a.m. to 6:00 p.m.	OFF	OFF	OFF
7:00 a.m.: Breakfast and take Ella to school 8:00 a.m.: Write in journal/Pick Tweaks of the Week	7:00 a.m.: Breakfast and take Ella to school 8:00 a.m.: Write in journal			7:00 a.m.: Breakfast and take Ella to school 8:00 a.m.: Write in journal	7:00 a.m.: Breakfast with Ella 9:00 a.m.: Skiing with Ella	8:00 a.m.: Write in journal
10:00 a.m.: Gym 12:00 p.m.: Open 529 account for Ella's education 2:00 p.m.: Call to schedule physical 4:00 p.m.: Pick up Ella after school	10:00 a.m.: Gym 12:00 p.m.: Shop for Super Bowl party. Clean the house and fix the food.	12:00 p.m.: Lunch (packed at home)	12:00 p.m.: Lunch (packed at home)	10 a.m.: Gym 12:00 p.m.: Meet with accountant to set up LLC; register URL 4:00 p.m.: Pick up Ella after school		10:00 a.m.: Gym 12:00 p.m.: Finish getting ready for party
6:00 p.m.: Dinner with Ella 9:00 p.m.: Dim lights and put on glasses before bed 11:00 p.m.: To bed	7:00 p.m.: Dinner and pack lunch 8:00 p.m.: Dim lights and put on glasses before bed 10:00 p.m.: To bed	7:00 p.m.: Dinner and pack lunch 8:00 p.m.: Dim lights and put on glasses before bed 8:15 p.m.: Call Cynthia's friend and invite to Super Bowl party 10:00 p.m.: To bed	7:00 p.m.: Dinner and pack lunch 8:00 p.m.: Download program to automatically dim computer screen 9:00 p.m.: Dim lights and put on glasses before bed 11:00 p.m.: To bed	6:00 p.m.: Dinner with Ella 8:15 p.m.: Get Ella login info and look at her social sites with her 9:00 p.m.: Dim lights and put on glasses before bed 11:00 p.m.: To bed	6:00 p.m.: Dinner and drive Ella home 9:00 p.m.: Dim lights and put on glasses before bed 11:00 p.m.: To bed	5:00 p.m.: Super Bowl party 9:00 p.m.: Dim lights and put on glasses before bed 11:00 p.m.: To bed

Priority List

✓ Connect with Ella either by phone, text, or e-mail twice a day

✓ Be more aware when I'm at the gym of women who make an effort to connect

Phase 3: Review and Revise

After four weeks, the *Tweak It* practice has proven Jeff's theory right—when you work an irregular schedule that changes week to week, you need a routine if you want to stay healthy and if you want what matters to you to happen. His sleep is much improved, as is his diet, although he's struggling to eat two healthy meals a day. He will make healthy eating a key area of his *Tweak It* focus next month.

The Super Bowl party was a success. He feels good about his relationship with his daughter and will continue to pursue opportunities to date. The softball league he signed up for starts in a couple of months, and he hopes to meet new people. Now that his handyman business is up and running, he's going to start marketing and booking jobs. This will add a whole new element to his work+life fit, but with *Tweak It* he thinks he can handle it all.

What would he change about the *Tweak It* Practice?

TWEAK IT *SNAPSHOT CALENDAR AND PRIORITY LIST:*

Add a third Google Calendar for his handyman business.

TWEAK IT *DEFINITION OF SUCCESS:*

He would change it to: (1) continue to eat healthier, (2) grow the handyman business and make money, and (3) meet new people

STANDARD TWEAKS:

Add "Dim the lights and wear glasses two hours before bed." Both steps helped him get to sleep, and he wants to continue them to see if it gets even better.

Chapter 9

Denise's Tweak It *Practice*

Denise's Tweak It *Snapshot:*

Denise is an administrator who has worked for the same community college for twenty-five years. Her primary responsibility for the past five years has been to support the school's board of trustees. Because she's an early riser, she typically puts in a few minutes checking e-mails and getting her to-do list in order for the day before getting ready for work and arriving in the office around 8:30 or 9:00 a.m. At fifty-seven years old, she is starting to think about an interim, or encore, career she'd like to pursue before she retires completely. All was going as planned until she got the call from her mother.

Denise's father has been diagnosed with early-stage Alzheimer's disease. At eighty-three years old, he had lived an otherwise healthy independent life with Denise's mother, who is the same age. Denise is one of three children. She has a brother, Charlie, and a sister, Alice, both of whom live in other states. Because she lives only an hour away from her parents, Denise has found herself taking on the primary responsibility for helping them navigate this difficult turn of events.

Still in the early stages of getting a handle of what this means for her and her parents, Denise tries to leave work by 5:30 or 6:00 p.m. in order to be home in time to check in with them. And for the past couple of months, she has spent almost every Saturday night at her parents' house to give her mother a break. To get a head start on her week in case issues come up with her parents, she tries to get work done on Sunday afternoons.

As soon as she found out about the diagnosis, she joined a local Alzheimer's support group and finds the weekly meetings very helpful. Although she's only attended them for a few weeks, she's learned enough to know how important it is for caregivers to value their own health and well-being. To that end, Denise is trying to sustain her exercise program and has added stress management techniques to her daily routine. One top priority is her relationship with Pat, the person she started dating a few months ago after another long-term relationship ended.

She knows she can't do everything and needs help, but she's not sure what that looks like yet.

Phase 1: Get Started

DENISE'S TWEAK IT SNAPSHOT CALENDAR AND PRIORITY LIST:

While the university uses a shared calendar system, Denise prefers tracking her everyday work+life fit with an Excel spreadsheet.

DENISE'S DEFINITION OF TWEAK IT SUCCESS:

For the first month working with the *Tweak It* practice, Denise would be satisfied if she were able to:

- get a clearer handle on what her father's elder-care needs were, how they can be handled, and by whom;

- get help with other personal responsibilities, like her house and car, so that she can put her time and energy elsewhere;
- maintain her health and manage her stress;
- sustain her relationship with Pat; and
- continue to explore her next-stage, preretirement career options.

DENISE'S STANDARD TWEAKS:

The period during the week that she seems to have the time to think and plan most consistently is Sunday evening at 7 p.m., after visiting her parents and before the week begins. She'll use that time to pick her Tweaks of the Week.

Denise would like to continue her weekly fitness routine of swimming three times a week at the YMCA pool. And she feels, at least for now, that her nightly calls to her parents are important to continue.

In terms of new standard tweaks to add, she and Pat have decided to schedule a standing dinner date for Wednesday night right after work and another evening together on Fridays. Before her father's diagnosis they could be more spontaneous, but they both agree that a more formal schedule is important, at least for the next few weeks. When she visits her parents on Saturday nights and they go to bed early, Denise finds that she has more time to read. Therefore, once a week, she'd like to wander in the college library for a few minutes and pick a new book for the weekend.

Finally, because she is at her parents' house every Saturday night, Denise is unable to attend services at her house of worship on Sunday mornings. Instead she's decided to use her bus ride to work as a time to meditate and to go through her prayer list. Both practices help her manage her growing stress. In case she has an unexpected issue with her parents, she'll spend a couple of hours late Sunday afternoon getting a handle on her schedule for the coming week at work.

Phase 2: Pick Your Unique Tweaks of the Week

DENISE'S TWEAKS OF THE WEEK—WEEK 1:

Denise's goal during the first week of the *Tweak It* practice is to get the ball rolling in the three main areas on which she wants to focus. First, elder care. That means scheduling a meeting for later in the month with her parents and her siblings to sit down and discuss a plan. She also wants to research possible geriatric-care managers who could take on the local logistics of the care for Denise and her siblings.

She's become aware of the many resources that Alzheimer's families require and of the nonprofits that work hard to provide those services, often under financial pressure. She wants to figure out how she can best support one or more of these organizations with either her money or her time. Finally, she would like to find technology that can help her communicate with her family and manage the care more effectively and efficiently from a distance.

The other area of focus is organizing and getting help with the maintenance of her house and car. And she'd like to sustain the momentum of her encore career exploration. With these goals in mind for the week, Denise records the following Tweaks of the Week in her *Tweak It* worksheet:

Denise's Tweak It Worksheet—Week 1

Standard Tweaks	Action or Priority	Target Date/Time	Communicate/Coordinate Plan
Pick Tweaks of the Week	Action	Sun., 7:00 p.m.	Devote the last hour of my Sunday work period to picking my tweaks
Swim in the YMCA pool three times a week	Action	Mon. and Wed., 6:30 a.m.; Fri., 7:00 a.m.	
Check in with my mother and father every day	Priority	Weekday evenings at dinner time; Sat., overnight	Schedule meetings to end at 5:00 p.m. so I can be out of the office by 5:30 p.m.
Every Wednesday, have dinner with Pat	Action	Wed., 6:00 p.m.	
Once a week wander to library and pick a book	Action	Fri., 1:00 p.m.	Get recommendations from friends during the week
Use bus ride to work to meditate and to go through my prayer list	Action	Every weekday morning	

Unique Tweaks of the Week	Action or Priority	Target Date/Time	Communicate/Coordinate Plan
Think about how I want to support an Alzheimer's nonprofit—money and/or time?	Action	Tues., 8:00 p.m.	Write pros and cons of both options

Task	Type	Time	Notes
Schedule a visit to ask Mom and Dad how they want to be cared for and author their end-of-life preferences. Ask brother and sister to come too.	Action	Mon., 7:00 p.m.	First discuss the meeting with my parents, and if they are in agreement call Alice and Charlie to schedule
Research potential geriatric care managers in parents' town	Action	Thurs., 12:00 p.m.	Check with local elder-care attorney
Send an e-mail to three friends in the neighborhood who have cleaning help and ask for referral	Action	Sun., 2:00 p.m.	Decide how often I want help
Go to PopularMechanics.com and download the Autumn Home Checklist*	Action	Sat., 11:00 a.m.	
Clean car inside and outside	Action	Sat., 9:00 a.m.	Go right from swimming to car wash
Think about how I want technology to help me communicate regarding care	Action	Sat., 8:30 p.m.	Ask friends in Alzheimer's support group what they do/use
Review the Encore Career site**	Action	Sun., 4:00 p.m.	Write down stories that are relevant and inspiring

* Popular Mechanics's *Autumn Home Checklist* can be found at *www.popularmechanics.com/home/improvement/ outdoor-projects/394316?click=main_sr.*
** *The Encore Career site can be found at www.encore.org.*

After Denise lists her Tweaks of the Week in her *Tweak It* worksheet, she inputs them into her *Tweak It* calendar and priority list on Excel:

Denise's Tweak It Calendar and Priority List—Week 1

Monday	Tuesday	Wednesday	Thursday	Friday	Saturday	Sunday
Work 6:30 a.m. at home; 8:30 a.m. to 5:30 p.m. in office	Work 9:00 a.m. to 6:00 p.m. in office	Work 6:30 a.m. at home; 8:30 a.m. to 5:30 p.m. in office	Work 9:00 a.m. to 6:00 p.m. in office	Work 6:30 a.m. at home; 8:30 a.m. to 5:30 p.m. in office	Work 4:00 p.m. to 8:00 p.m. at home	8:00 a.m.: Meditate and go through prayer list on bus ride
6:30 a.m.: Swim 8:30 a.m.: Meditate and go through prayer list on bus ride	8:00 a.m.: Meditate and go through prayer list on bus ride	6:30 a.m.: Swim 8:30 a.m.: Meditate and go through prayer list on bus ride	8:00 a.m.: Meditate and go through prayer list on bus ride	7:00 a.m.: Swim		
12:00 p.m.: Research and call geriatric caregivers	5:30 p.m.: Connect with parents	12:00 p.m.: Research and call geriatric caregivers	1:00 p.m.: Wander library and get book	9:00 a.m.: Clean car inside and outside 11:00 a.m.: Download Autumn Home Checklist 3:00 p.m.: To parents' overnight	12:00 p.m.: Back from parents 2:00 p.m.: E-mail neighbors to get referrals for cleaning help 4:00 p.m.: Review Encore Career site	7:00 p.m.: Dinner and connect with parents; schedule family meeting with them 8:00 p.m.: Call brother and sister regarding family meeting 9:30 p.m.: To bed
7:00 p.m.: Dinner and connect with parents 8:00 p.m.: Think about best way to support Alzheimer's nonprofit 9:30 p.m.: To bed	6:00 p.m.: Dinner with Pat 9:30 p.m.: To bed	6:30 p.m.: Dinner and connect with parents 7:30 p.m.: Local Alzheimer's support group 9:30 p.m.: To bed	7:00 p.m.: Evening with Pat By 10:30 p.m.: To bed	8:30 p.m.: Think about how tech can help coordination with family 10:00 p.m.: To bed	7:00 p.m.: Pick Tweaks of the Week 9:30 p.m.: To bed	

DENISE'S TWEAKS OF THE WEEK—WEEK 2

Denise was making good progress with her tweaks last week until her mother called on Thursday night to say that her father had fallen down and they were at the hospital. Instead of leaving for her support group meeting, Denise drove to the hospital and stayed with her mother until her father was discharged. She took them home, spent the night, and commuted the hour to work the next morning. She had hoped to stay at her own home on Friday night and go back to her parents Saturday, as scheduled. But when she called that afternoon, she could tell that her mother was overwhelmed. Denise drove back to her parents on Friday after work and stayed until Sunday. As a result, she didn't accomplish a number of tweaks she had planned, including time with Pat and getting her house and car maintenance in order. That would have to happen this week.

By Sunday afternoon, her parents seemed settled, and Denise was able to go home. As she sat in her kitchen thinking about her tweaks for the coming week, she realized how important it was for her to achieve her *Tweak It* goals for the month. She'd gotten a taste of how quickly the situation with her parents could go bad. She had no time to lose to get both her and their support systems in order.

Denise considered what steps she wanted to take this week and wrote the following Tweaks of the Week in her *Tweak It* worksheet:

Denise's Tweak It Worksheet—Week 2

Standard Tweaks	Action or Priority	Target Date/Time	Communicate/Coordinate Plan
Pick Tweaks of the Week	Action	Sun., 7 p.m.	Devote the last hour of my Sunday work period to picking my tweaks
Swim in the YMCA pool three times a week	Action	Tues. and Thurs., 6:30 a.m.; Sat., 7:00 a.m.	
Check in with my mother and father every day	Priority	Weekdays every night at dinner; Sat., overnight	Schedule meetings to end at 5:00 p.m. so that I can be out of the office by 5:30 p.m.
Every Wednesday, have dinner with Pat	Action	Wed., 6:00 p.m.	
Once a week wander to library and pick a book	Action	Fri., 1:00 p.m.	Get recommendations from friends during the week
Use bus ride to meditate and to go through my prayer list	Action	Every weekday morning	

Unique Tweaks of the Week	Action or Priority	Target Date/Time	Communicate/Coordinate Plan
Ask members of Alzheimer's support group about favorite nonprofit organizations	Action	Thurs., 7:30 p.m.	Bring the names of a couple of groups I've identified already to get their thoughts

Download *Five Wishes*, the end-of-life issues worksheet, for visit with Mom and Dad. Fill it out myself and send link to brother and sister so they can complete it.*	Action	Sat., 10:00 a.m.	Print out two hard copies to bring with me to the meeting—one for Mom and one for Dad.
Review online customer reviews and references of cleaning help referrals, if available	Action	Mon., 7:30 p.m.	
Download *Popular Mechanics* Autumn Home Maintenance checklist and schedule furnace tune-up	Action	Tues., 2 p.m.: schedule; Sat., 11:00 a.m.: service	
Check car's tire pressure and fluid levels	Action	Wed., 6:00 p.m.: drop off at station; Fri., 7:00 p.m.: pick up	Drive car to work on Wednesday
Car wash inside and outside	Action	Sat., 1:00 p.m.	
Go to www.digitwirl.com to research technologies that can help me communicate with my family better	Action	Sat., 8:00 p.m.	Remember to bring laptop to parents' and ask Pat to borrow his mobile Wi-Fi card
Join the Encore Careers group on LinkedIn.com and follow them on social media	Action	Sun., 4:00 p.m.	

* *The* Five Wishes *worksheet can be found at www.agingwithdignity.org.*

After Denise identified the small activities and priorities she wanted to achieve over the next seven days, she put them into her *Tweak It* snapshot calendar and priority list system in Excel:

Denise's Tweak It Snapshot Calendar and Priority List—Week 2

Monday	Tuesday	Wednesday	Thursday	Friday	Saturday	Sunday
Work 6:30 a.m. at home; 8:30 a.m. to 5:30 p.m. in office	Work 9:00 a.m. to 6:00 p.m. in office	Work 6:30 a.m. at home; 8:30 a.m. to 5:30 p.m. in office	Work 9:00 a.m. to 6:00 p.m. in office	Work 6:30 a.m. at home; 8:30 a.m. to 5:30 p.m. in office		Work 4:00 p.m. to 8:00 p.m. at home
8:00 a.m.: Meditate and go through prayer list on bus ride	6:30 a.m.: Swim 8:30 a.m.: Meditate and go through prayer list on bus ride	Drive to work	6:30 a.m.: Swim 8:30 a.m.: Meditate and go through prayer list on bus ride	8:00 a.m.: Meditate and go through prayer list on bus ride	7:00 a.m.: Swim	
	2:00 p.m.: Download Autumn Home Maintenance checklist; schedule furnace checkup for Saturday	5:30 p.m.: Connect with parents before leaving work		1:00 p.m.: Wander to library to get book	10:00 a.m.: Download *Five Wishes* and complete; send link to brother and sister so they can complete it before family meeting 11:00 a.m.: Furnace checkup 3:00 p.m.: To parents overnight	12:00 p.m.: Back from parents 4:00 p.m.: Join Encore Career LinkedIn group
7:00 p.m.: Dinner and connect with parents 7:30 p.m.: Check references; read online reviews of potential cleaning help 9:30 p.m.: To bed	7:00 p.m.: Dinner and connect with parents 9:30 p.m.: To bed	6:00 p.m.: Dinner with Pat; drop off car at service station 9:30 p.m.: To bed	6:30 p.m.: Dinner and connect with parents 7:30 p.m.: Local Alzheimer's support group; ask members for their favorite Alzheimer's nonprofits 9:30 p.m.: To bed	7:00 p.m.: Evening with Pat; pick up car at service station To bed by 10:30 p.m.	8:00 p.m.: Research communication technology 10:00 p.m.: To bed	7:00 p.m.: Pick Tweaks of the Week

DENISE'S TWEAKS OF THE WEEK—WEEK 3

While all was calm with Denise's parents this week, work was busier than usual. The board of trustees requested a report on an urgent matter that they needed to resolve quickly. Denise had to stay at work late on Wednesday. She missed her regular check-in with her parents and she couldn't have dinner with Pat. He was also unable to help her take the car to the service station. Otherwise, she accomplished the other Tweaks of the Week she had planned. Even though there have been some activities and priorities that haven't happened, Denise feels she is making progress, especially with her elder-care planning.

Regarding elder care, this week Denise must get the financial information she needs from her parents to come up with a care budget for them. And she wants to find the last piece of information she needs before she decides which Alzheimer's nonprofit to support.

Her goal for her car and home maintenance is to set up interviews with two potential housecleaning services, schedule leaf removal, and review the car's owner's manual. Her car has almost a hundred thousand miles on it, and before she reschedules the service appointment she hopes to understand what else needs to be checked. Also, because she's driven her car more in the last two months than in the previous year, she wants to set up an account to save for repair costs. Every month, she's going to deposit what she used to pay in a monthly car payment. If she doesn't use the money for repairs, she'll use it for a down payment on her next car.

Finally, she's decided that Skype will help her communicate more effectively with both her brother and sister regarding her parents' care. And she will continue her encore career exploration by reading a book on the topic by Marc Freedman, founder and CEO of Civic Ventures and Encore Careers. Here are the tweaks she chose for the coming week:

Denise's Tweak It Worksheet—Week 3

Standard Tweaks	Action or Priority	Target Date/Time	Communicate/Coordinate Plan
Pick Tweaks of the Week	Action	Sun., 7:00 p.m.	Devote last hour of Sunday work period to picking tweaks
Swim in the YMCA pool three times a week	Action	Tues. and Thurs., 6:30 a.m.; Sat., 7:00 a.m.	
Check in with my mother and father every day	Priority	Weekdays every night at dinner; Sat., overnight	Schedule meetings to end at 5:00 p.m. so that I can be out of the office by 5:30 p.m.
Every Wednesday, have dinner with Pat	Action	Wed., 6:00 p.m.	
Once a week wander to library and pick a book	Action	Fri., 1:00 p.m.	Get Marc Freedman's encore career book, *The Big Shift: Navigating the New Stage beyond Midlife*
Use bus ride to work to meditate and to go through my prayer list	Action	Every weekday morning	

Unique Tweaks of the Week	Action or Priority	Target Date/Time	Communicate/Coordinate Plan
Contact two or three Alzheimer's nonprofits to request financial information	Action	Mon., 12:00 p.m.	
Get copies of parents' financial records and long-term care policy to determine the available budget for care	Action	Sat., 5:00 p.m.	Take to Staples to get copies
Set up interviews with at least two potential housecleaners	Action	Sat., 11:00 a.m.	
Schedule leaf removal from gutters	Action	Tues., 1:00 p.m.	
Review owner's manual to confirm car's service schedule	Action	Mon., 8:00 p.m.	If not in glove compartment, find PDF of it on web
Set up account to save amount I used to pay for car payment to cover annual car repair expenses	Action	Sat., 9:00 a.m.	Have the bank link to other online accounts
Buy a webcam for my computer, schedule time for my nephew to set it up and to help me create a Skype account	Action	Sun., 3:00 p.m.	Print out computer specifications to make sure I get the right camera

Having outlined the specific tweaks she wanted to accomplish over the next week, Denise input them into her calendar and priority list system:

Denise's Tweak It Calendar and Priority List—Week 3

Monday	Tuesday	Wednesday	Thursday	Friday	Saturday	Sunday
Work 6:30 a.m. at home; 8:30 a.m. to 5:30 p.m. in office	Work 9:00 a.m. to 6:00 p.m. in office	Work 6:30 a.m. at home; 8:30 a.m. to 5:30 p.m. in office	Work 9:00 a.m. to 6:00 p.m. in office	Work 6:30 a.m. at home; 8:30 a.m. to 5:30 p.m. in office		Work 4:00 p.m. to 8:00 p.m. at home
8:00 a.m.: Meditate and go through prayer list on bus ride	6:30 a.m.: Swim 8:30 a.m.: Meditate and go through prayer list on bus ride	8:00 a.m.: Meditate and go through prayer list on bus ride	6:30 a.m.: Swim 8:30 a.m.: Meditate and go through prayer list on bus ride	8:00 a.m.: Meditate and go through prayer list on bus ride	7:00 a.m.: Swim	
12:00 p.m.: E-mail two Alzheimer's nonprofits to request financial information	1:00 p.m.: Schedule leaf removal from gutters	5:30 p.m.: Connect with parents		1:00 p.m.: Go to library to get Marc Freedman's encore career book	9:00 a.m.: Set up car repair account 11:00 a.m.: Set up interviews with housecleaners 3:00 p.m.: To parents overnight	12:00 p.m.: Back from parents 2:00 p.m.: Schedule time for nephew to visit to install camera and set up Skype 3:00 p.m.: Buy computer camera
7:00 p.m.: Dinner and connect with parents 8:00 p.m.: Review car manual 9:30 p.m.: To bed	7:00 p.m.: Dinner and connect with parents 9:30 p.m.: To bed	6:00 p.m.: Dinner with Pat 9:30 p.m.: To bed	6:30 p.m.: Dinner and connect with parents 7:30 p.m.: Local Alzheimer's support group 9:30 p.m.: To bed	7:00 p.m.: Evening with Pat To bed by 10:30 p.m.	5:00 p.m.: Get copies of parents' records 10:00 p.m.: To bed	7:00 p.m.: Tweaks of the Week 9:30 p.m.: To bed

Priority List

✓ Read Marc Freedman's book *The Big Shift: Navigating the New Stage beyond Midlife*

DENISE'S TWEAKS OF THE WEEK—WEEK 4

Luck was on Denise's side this week both at work and with her parents. She was able to catch her breath, reconnect with Pat, swim, sleep, meditate/pray, eat well, and get closer to getting help with the house. She needed to reenergize because this week she has to prepare for the family meeting with her parents and her siblings on Saturday. Denise will pull together the financial and caregiving information she's gathered and present the caregiving budget and local support system options. She also plans to choose an Alzheimer's nonprofit that will receive her donation.

She hopes to be ready to decide on a housecleaning service by the end of the week and to have snow removal for the winter confirmed. As far as Skype is concerned, her nephew is visiting to set it up, and she's scheduled test calls with her brother and sister. Finally, even though it may be too much, she's decided to sign up for an Encore Career summit being held at the college in two months. It's something to aspire to, and the worst that can happen is she has to cancel.

Denise's Tweak It Worksheet—Week 4

Standard Tweaks	Action or Priority	Target Date/Time	Communicate/Coordinate Plan
Pick Tweaks of the Week	Action	Sun., 7:00 p.m.	Nephew visiting; pick tweaks an hour later this week
Swim in the college pool three times a week	Action	Tues. and Thurs., 6:30 a.m.; Sat., 7:00 a.m.	
Check in with my mother and father every day	Priority	Weekdays every night at dinner; Sat., overnight	Schedule meetings to end at 5:00 p.m. so that I can be out of the office by 5:30 p.m.
Every Wednesday, have dinner with Pat	Action	Wed., 6:00 p.m.	
Once a week wander to library and pick a book	Action	Not this week	Get recommendations for friends during the week
Use bus ride to work to meditate and to go through my prayer list	Action	Every weekday morning	

Unique Tweaks of the Week	Action or Priority	Target Date/Time	Communicate/Coordinate Plan
Review information nonprofits sent, choose one, and send donation	Action	Sat., 10:00 a.m.	

Task	Type	Time	Notes
Create a document outlining parents' financial situation and care budget to discuss at the meeting with entire family	Action	Mon., 7:30 p.m.; Tues., 7:30 p.m.; Sat., 11 a.m.	Have Diane, the leader of the Alzheimer's group, review the document and tell me her thoughts on my recommendations
Set up interviews with potential house-cleaners	Action	Mon., 12:00 p.m.	Create list of questions to ask before the interviews
Confirm contract with snow removal service for the winter	Action	Tues., 1:00 p.m.	
Nephew visits to set up Skype; and schedule test calls with my sister and brother	Action	Sun., 2:00 p.m.: Set-up; Sun., 4:00 p.m.: Test calls	
Watch Skype online tutorials	Action	Fri., 1:00 p.m.	
Sign up to attend Encore Careers workshop being sponsored by the university's alumni organization	Action	Wed., 9:00 a.m.	Find out deadline for refund in case I have to cancel

Once Denise identified the small activities and priorities she wanted to accomplish over the next seven days, she put the following Tweaks of the Week into her *Tweak It* snapshot calendar and priority list in Excel:

Denise's Tweak It Snapshot Calendar and Priority List—Week 4

Monday	Tuesday	Wednesday	Thursday	Friday	Saturday	Sunday
Work 6:30 a.m. at home; 8:30 a.m. to 5:30 p.m. in office	Work 9:00 a.m. to 6:00 p.m. in office	Work 6:30 a.m. at home; 8:30 a.m. to 5:30 p.m. in office	Work 9:00 a.m. to 6:00 p.m. in office	Work 6:30 a.m. at home; 8:30 a.m. to 5:30 p.m. in office		Work 4:00 p.m. to 8:00 p.m. at home
8:00 a.m.: Meditate and go through prayer list on bus ride	6:30 a.m.: Swim 8:30 a.m.: Meditate and go through prayer list on bus ride	8:00 a.m.: Meditate and go through prayer list on bus ride	6:30 a.m.: Swim 8:30 a.m.: Meditate and go through prayer list on bus ride	8:00 a.m.: Meditate and go through prayer list on bus ride	7:00 a.m.: Swim	
12:00 p.m.: Arrange interviews with final two housecleaning help candidates	1:00 p.m.: Confirm contract for snow removal in winter	9:00 a.m.: Sign up for Encore Career workshop 5:30 p.m.: Connect with parents before leaving work		1:00 p.m.: Watch online Skype tutorials	10:00 a.m.: Send donation to Alzheimer's nonprofit 11:00 a.m.: Finalize document outlining parents' finances, care budget, and geriatric advisor options 3:00 p.m.: To parents for family meeting with brother and sister to discuss finances, care, and end-of-life	12:00 p.m.: Back from parents 2:00 p.m.: Nephew arrives; installs Skype and camera 4:00 p.m.: Test Skype call with brother and sister
7:00 p.m.: Dinner and connect with parents 7:30 p.m.: Outline parents' financial picture 9:30 p.m.: To bed	7:00 p.m.: Dinner and connect with parents 7:30 p.m.: Develop care budget for parents 9:30 p.m.: To bed	6:00 p.m.: Dinner with Pat 9:30 p.m.: To bed	6:30 p.m.: Dinner and connect with parents 7:30 p.m.: Local Alzheimer's support group 9:30 p.m.: To bed	7:00 p.m.: Evening with Pat By 10:30 p.m.: To bed	10:00 p.m.: To bed	5:00 p.m.: Dinner with nephew 8:00 p.m.: Pick Tweaks of the Week 9:30 p.m.: To bed

Phase 3: Review and Revise

The meeting with her family went well, and everyone agreed that Denise couldn't sustain the level of care she was providing to her parents while working full-time. The family hired a local geriatric-care manager who would coordinate the care locally and communicate with Denise and her siblings. Her brother and sister agreed to share the responsibility for making the daily check-in calls with Denise. That meant she had to call only one or two nights a week. They all agreed to hire a part-time nurse to spend two Saturdays a month with their parents. Denise would go down one weekend a month, and her brother and sister would share responsibility for the other one.

Knowing that she could be called to help her parents on a moment's notice, Denise talked to her boss about getting a laptop and Internet access that would allow her to telework when needed.

Even though it wasn't an easy month, Denise feels the *Tweak It* practice helped her to take the best care of herself possible, see Pat regularly, choose someone to help her clean the house, address her other house and car maintenance issues, and continue to research her encore career.

TWEAK IT *SNAPSHOT CALENDAR AND PRIORITY LIST:*

For Denise, the Excel spreadsheet works well. She's now sharing it each week with her mother and her siblings so they know (and can respect) her schedule.

TWEAK IT *DEFINITION OF SUCCESS:*

Now that her elder-care and house maintenance supports are in place, Denise wants to make her ongoing health and stress management, her relationship with Pat, and her encore career research her primary *Tweak It* goals.

STANDARD TWEAKS:

No changes.

Chapter 10

Pete's Tweak It *Practice*

Pete's Tweak It *Snapshot:*

For Pete and his wife, Amy, both in their late twenties, this past year was full of major personal and professional transitions. One year ago, Amy gave birth to their first child, a boy named Tommy. Shortly after returning from her maternity leave, Amy was offered a promotion. It meant a transfer to Seattle from their home in Chicago. Pete saw the move as an opportunity to start the business he'd wanted to launch with a former business colleague, Mark, who lives in New York City.

They decided to take the plunge. Pete quit his job, and for the past six months he's taken on the primary responsibility for getting the family settled in Seattle and for being the go-to parent for Tommy. He also started to set up the business with Mark.

The only way to describe his work schedule is "whenever, and wherever." Mark and Pete have used the time difference to their advantage. Mark handles business from 8 a.m. to 5 p.m. EST, with Pete checking in as needed, and then Pete takes over at 2 p.m. PST (5 p.m. EST) until 12 a.m. PST (3 a.m. EST). Together they have all of the time zones covered, but as the business grows, Mark needs Pete to be more available during some of his main East Coast work hours.

Two college students have shared babysitting duties for Tommy every afternoon, which allows Pete to focus on work consistently from 2 p.m. to 6 p.m. Monday through Friday. Because he's a night owl, Pete reengages again after Tommy goes to bed, until midnight. During the weekend, Amy takes over for most of Saturday, which lets Pete get caught up. However, two months ago, his "always on" work schedule became so crazy that he and Amy finally instituted "Tech-free Sunday." It's restored some sanity to Pete's life and showed him the benefits of placing structure around his extreme work and life flexibility, and he realizes he needs more.

Now that Tommy is a year old, and Amy is more comfortable in her job and has more work flexibility to help with Tommy, Pete's decided to use the *Tweak It* practice to establish a more consistent routine at work and in their lives over the next month.

Phase 1: Get Started

PETE'S TWEAK IT *SNAPSHOT CALENDAR AND PRIORITY LIST:*

The iCalendar is the system both he and Mark use, and he can coordinate with Amy as well. His priority list is the app called Remember the Milk (www.rememberthemilk.com).

PETE'S DEFINITION OF TWEAK IT *SUCCESS:*

Pete knows there's no balance because the work demands of his new venture are as unpredictable as the needs of his young son. However, he can make some order out of the chaos. Specifically, he will feel *Tweak It* has been successful if he has:

- found a full-time caregiver for Tommy,
- established a household routine that works for everyone,
- reconnected with his wife because they often feel like two ships passing in the night,
- become part of their community, and
- joined a local network of entrepreneurs.

PETE'S STANDARD TWEAKS:

Because he is at his most productive at night, Pete decides to pick his Tweaks of the Week on Monday nights at 10 p.m. before he goes to bed.

Jogging with Tommy in the stroller for thirty minutes about three times a week and "Tech-free" Sundays are the two activities he wants to try to continue.

The two new standard tweaks he'd like to add are: (1) having a family dinner once on the weekends and once during the week, and (2) coordinating and sharing Tommy's bath- and bedtime routine with Amy. Right now, it's done by whoever happens to be there, which wastes everyone's time, including Tommy's.

Phase 2: Pick Your Unique Tweaks of the Week

PETE'S TWEAKS OF THE WEEK—WEEK 1:

Because it will involve the most legwork and is such an important decision, Pete decides to focus his first week of unique tweaks on getting full-time, backup, and weekend child care for Tommy. He'll start by researching various child-care options in the area, posting a job description for a sitter online and in town, and visiting a couple of local centers. Later in the week, Pete will allow time to follow up with anyone who responds to the posting. Outreach to the neighbors early in the week should provide names of possible weekend babysitters. Pete will book a night out with his wife to test how comfortable Tommy is with one of them.

Pete's Tweak It Worksheet—Week 1:

Standard Tweaks	Action or Priority	Target Date/Time	Communicate/Coordinate Plan
Pick Tweaks of the Week	Action	Mon., 10:00 p.m.	Confirm with Mark no calls with overseas customers/suppliers after 10:00 p.m. on Monday
Jog with Tommy in the stroller for thirty minutes three times a week	Action	Mon., Wed., Fri., 8:30 a.m.	Let Mark know I won't be able to respond to e-mails from 8:30 a.m. to 9:30 a.m.
Have a Tech-free Sunday	Action	Sunday	Answer pending, urgent e-mails Saturday
Have family dinner together twice a week	Action	Wed., 7:00 p.m. and Sun., 5:30 p.m.	On weekday, make sure any meeting/call ends an hour before dinner; have Amy put the dates and times on her calendar as well
Coordinate evening bath/bedtime routine coverage with Amy	Action	Mon., Wed., Fri., and Sat.: cover	Coordinate preferred nights with Amy on Sunday

Unique Tweaks of the Week	Action or Priority	Target Date/Time	Communicate/Coordinate Plan
Research the child-care options in the area online and ask neighbors	Action	Mon., 11:00 a.m.	Get Tommy down for his morning nap on time. Tell Mark I'm not available from 11:00 a.m. to 1:00 p.m.
Download example of a child-care job posting from Care.com and write description	Action	Tues., 12:00 p.m.	Get Tommy down for his morning nap on time. Tell Mark I'm not available from 11:00 a.m. to 1:00 p.m.
Post the job in the local paper, in the library, and on websites	Action	Wed., 11:00 a.m.	Get Tommy down for his morning nap on time. Tell Mark I'm not available from 11:00 a.m. to 1:00 p.m.
Ask neighbors for weekend babysitters	Priority		
Schedule a dinner out with wife and book one of the recommended weekend sitters for next Saturday	Action	Thurs., 10:00 a.m.	Ask Amy where she'd like to go on Wednesday during family dinner
Follow up with people who've responded to the child-care ad and schedule time for initial phone interview	Action	Fri., 11:00 a.m.	Get Tommy down for his morning nap on time. Tell Mark I'm not available from 11:00 a.m. to 1:00 p.m.
Schedule visit and check out local child-care center	Action	Thurs., 8:30 a.m.	Research what questions are important to ask and what to look for

After Pete outlined the child-care-related tweaks he wanted to make happen during the week in his *Tweak It* worksheet, he put them into his *Tweak It* snapshot calendar and priority list:

Pete's Tweak It Snapshot Calendar and Priority List—Week 1

Monday	Tuesday	Wednesday	Thursday	Friday	Saturday	Sunday
Work whenever: 2:00 p.m. to 6:00 p.m.; 8:30 p.m. to 12:00 a.m.	Work whenever: 2:00 p.m. to 6:00 p.m.; 8:00 p.m. to 12:00 a.m.	Work whenever: 2:00 p.m. to 6:00 p.m.; 9:00 p.m. to 12:00 a.m.	Work whenever: 2:00 p.m. to 6:00 p.m.; 8:00 p.m. to 12:00 a.m.	Work whenever: 2:00 p.m. to 6:00 p.m.	Work whenever: 10:00 a.m. to 1:00 p.m.; 3:00 p.m. to 6:00 p.m.	Tech-free Sunday
7:00 a.m.: Wake up 8:30 a.m.: Jog with stroller 11:00 a.m.: Research local child-care options 7:30 p.m.: In charge of bath/bedtime 10:00 p.m.: Pick Tweaks of the Week Midnight: To bed	7:00 a.m.: Wake up 8:30 a.m.: Visit local child-care center with Tommy and wife 12:00 p.m.: Download and write child-care job posting Midnight: To bed	7:00 a.m.: Wake up 8:30 a.m.: Jog with stroller 11:00 a.m.: Post child-care job description 7:00 p.m.: Family dinner 8:00 p.m.: In charge of bath/bedtime Midnight: To bed	7:00 a.m.: Wake up 10:00 a.m.: Pick Saturday night for dinner date with wife/call weekend sitter Midnight: To bed	7:00 a.m.: Wake up 8:30 a.m.: Jog with stroller 11:00 a.m.: Follow up with people who have responded to posting and set up interviews 7:30 p.m.: In charge of bath/bedtime Midnight: To bed	7:00 a.m.: Wake up Exact times TBD: Possible caregiver interviews 7:30 p.m.: In charge of bath/bedtime	Sleep in/Amy up with baby 5:30 p.m.: Family dinner

Priority List

✓ When I see neighbors, remember to ask about full-time and weekend babysitter referrals

PETE'S TWEAKS OF THE WEEK—WEEK 2

Because of an unexpected supplier issue that Mark needed Pete to help him with during Tommy's nap time on Tuesday, Pete wasn't able to draft the child-caregiver job description until later that night. But otherwise, Pete completed all of the child-care-related tweaks he had planned for the week. He's identified two possible full-time sitters and one child-care center. He wants both Amy and Tommy to meet the sitters and visit the center before he makes the final decision.

This week, he's going to turn his attention to establishing a more organized morning and evening household routine for handling the dishes, getting meals ready, cleaning up and doing the laundry. He's following the advice of Lorie Marrero, of The Clutter Diet™, who advises establishing one place in the house as the "destination station," where Amy's purse, his wallet, Tommy's diaper bag, the car keys, and so forth all go. She also recommends a morning routine she calls D-E-W™ (where you decide what's for dinner, empty the dishwasher, and put laundry in the washer), and an evening routine she calls Triple S™ (where you start the dishwasher, straighten up, and get everything set for the next day).

Pete will tie up personal financial loose ends, like making sure their car insurance is valid in Seattle, adding Tommy to their will, and rolling over his 401(k) from his previous job. And, finally, enjoy their first dinner out alone without Tommy.

Pete's Tweak It Worksheet—Week 2

Standard Tweaks	Action or Priority	Target Date/Time	Communicate/Coordinate Plan
Pick Tweaks of the Week	Action	Mon., 10:00 p.m.	Confirm with Mark no calls with overseas customers/suppliers after 10:00 p.m. on Monday
Jog with Tommy in the stroller for thirty minutes three times a week	Action	Mon., Wed., Fri., 8:30 a.m.	Let Mark know I won't be able to respond to e-mails from 8:30 a.m. to 9:30 a.m.
Have a tech-free Sunday	Action	Sunday	Answer pending, urgent e-mails Saturday
Have family dinner together twice a week	Action	Wed., 7 p.m. and Sun., 5:30 p.m.	On weekday, make sure any meeting/call ends an hour before dinner; have Amy put the dates and times on her calendar as well
Coordinate evening bath/bedtime routine coverage with Amy	Action	Tues., Thurs., Fri., and Sun., cover	Coordinate preferred nights with Amy on Sunday

Unique Tweaks of the Week	Action or Priority	Target Date/Time	Communicate/Coordinate Plan
Create a destination station	Action	Sun., 10:00 a.m.	Scout a couple of possible locations in the house beforehand

Follow morning D-E-W* routine: empty dishwasher, decide what's for dinner, put laundry in washer or dryer	Action	Every morning	Even though I will be tempted to check if there are e-mails from Mark, do this routine first, then check
Follow evening Triple S* routine: start the dishwasher, straighten up, get things set for tomorrow	Action	Every evening	Even though I will be tempted to check if there are important e-mails after dinner, do this routine first, then check
Review insurance policy to make sure I'm covered in a different state	Action	Mon., 11:00 a.m.	Get Tommy down for morning nap on time. Let Mark know I will not be available from 11:00 a.m. to 12:00 p.m.
Get recommendations for a local attorney to update my will to include Tommy	Action	Tues., 9:00 a.m.	
Roll over 401(k) from previous job	Action	Wed., 11:00 a.m.	Get Tommy down for morning nap on time. Let Mark know I will not be available from 11:00 a.m. to 12:00 p.m.
Go out to dinner with Amy	Action	Sat., 7:00 p.m.	Confirm sitter on Thursday
Interview two potential full-time baby-sitters and go back to child-care center with Amy and Tommy	Action	Thurs., 9:00 a.m.; Sat., 10:00 a.m.	Review pros and cons of candidates and center with Amy beforehand

*D-E-W and Triple S are trademarks of The Clutter Diet; www.clutterdiet.com.

After Pete had decided which tweaks he wanted to do this week in his *Tweak It* worksheet, he recorded them in his *Tweak It* snapshot calendar and priority list:

Pete's Tweak It Snapshot Calendar and Priority List—Week 2

Monday	Tuesday	Wednesday	Thursday	Friday	Saturday	Sunday
Work whenever: 2:00 p.m. to 6:00 p.m.; 8:30 p.m. to 12:00 a.m.	Work whenever: 2:00 p.m. to 6:00 p.m.; 8:00 p.m. to 12:00 a.m.	Work whenever: 2:00 p.m. to 6:00 p.m.; 9:00 p.m. to 12:00 a.m.	Work whenever: 2:00 p.m. to 6:00 p.m.; 8:00 p.m. to 12:00 a.m.	Work whenever: 2:00 p.m. to 6:00 p.m.	Work whenever: 10:00 a.m. to 1:00 p.m.; 3:00 p.m. to 6:00 p.m.	Tech-free Sunday
7:00 a.m.: Wake up 7:30 a.m.: D-E-W routine 8:30 a.m.: Jog with stroller	7:00 a.m.: Wake up 7:30 a.m.: D-E-W routine	7:00 a.m.: Wake up 7:30 a.m.: D-E-W routine 8:30 a.m.: Jog with stroller	7:00 a.m.: Wake up 7:30 a.m.: D-E-W routine	7:00 a.m.: Wake up 7:30 a.m.: D-E-W routine 8:30 a.m.: Jog with stroller	7:00 a.m.: Wake up 7:30 a.m.: D-E-W routine	Sleep in/Wife up with baby 7:30 a.m.: D-E-W routine
11:00 a.m.: Review insurance policies	9:00 a.m.: Get attorney referrals to update wills	11:00 a.m.: Roll over 401(k) plans from previous employer	9:00 a.m.: Visit child-care center again with Amy and Tommy		10:00 a.m.: Interview potential sitters in person with Amy and have them spend time with Tommy	10:00 a.m.: Set up destination station
6:30 p.m.: Dinner and Triple S routine 10:00 p.m.: Pick Tweaks of the Week 12:00 a.m.: To bed	6:30 p.m.: Dinner and Triple S routine 7:30 p.m.: In charge of bath/bedtime 12:00 a.m.: To bed	7:00 p.m.: Family dinner and Triple S routine 12:00 a.m.: To bed	6:30 p.m.: Dinner and Triple S routine 7:30 p.m.: In charge of bath/bedtime 12:00 a.m.: To bed	6:30 p.m.: Dinner and Triple S routine 7:30 p.m.: In charge of bath/bedtime 12:00 a.m.: To bed	7:00 p.m.: Out to dinner with Amy 11:00 p.m.: To bed	5:30 p.m.: Family dinner and Triple S routine 7:30 p.m.: In charge of bath/bedtime 11:00 p.m.: To bed

PETE'S TWEAKS OF THE WEEK—WEEK 3

Unfortunately instead of being routine, the financial loose end of rolling over his 401(k) turned out to be more complicated. Pete needs to open a new brokerage account and will have to deal with that next month.

Amy and Tommy met with the potential sitters and visited the child-care center. Everyone agreed that the best option for everyone was the center. Therefore, Pete will enroll Tommy this week to start next week.

While the D-E-W morning routine was a success, the evening Triple S routine didn't go as smoothly. It became clear to Pete and Amy after the third night that they needed to clearly split the clean-up duties and the bath/bedtime routine. Next week they will officially alternate the two responsibilities. With the destination station set up on a hutch they put by the front door, Pete hopes he'll lose less times scrambling to find his wallet, keys, and Tommy's favorite toy for the car.

This coming week is all about connecting with Amy and the community. Even though Tech-free Sundays and family dinner twice a week have given Pete and Amy more focused time together, he wants to do more. Amy's sister recently told her about an idea from relationship expert Esther Perel to help busy couples stay connected. She suggests surprising your partner with an adventure that you've planned and setting up a lovers' e-mail box that only the two of you use to communicate with each other. You can only send fun, loving messages; nothing about day-to-day management of the family. Pete's intrigued by the idea of a surprise adventure and is willing to give the e-mail box a shot because Amy likes the idea so much.

While he's met a number of neighbors over the past few months, Pete wants to formalize those relationships with a neighborhood contact list. And now that he will have more help with Tommy, he's hoping to plan a block party; but first he wants to see if people would be interested.

Pete's Tweak It Worksheet—Week 3

Standard Tweaks	Action or Priority	Target Date/Time	Communicate/Coordinate Plan
Pick Tweaks of the Week	Action	Mon., 10:00 p.m.	Confirm with Mark no calls with overseas customers/suppliers after 10:00 p.m. on Monday
Jog with Tommy in the stroller for thirty minutes three times a week	Action	Mon., Wed., Fri., 8:30 a.m.	Let Mark know I won't be able to respond to e-mails from 8:30 a.m. to 9:30 a.m.
Have a tech-free Sunday	Action	Sunday	Answer pending, urgent e-mails Saturday
Have family dinner together twice a week	Action	Wed., 7:00 p.m. and Sun., 5:30 p.m.	On weekday, make sure any meeting/call ends an hour before dinner; have Amy put the dates and times on her calendar as well
Coordinate Triple S and bath/bedtime routine coverage with Amy	Action	Mon., Wed., Fri.: cover bed/bath; Tues., Thurs., Sun.: cover Triple S	Coordinate preferred nights with Amy on Sunday

Unique Tweaks of the Week	Action or Priority	Target Date/Time	Communicate/Coordinate Plan
Create a neighborhood contact list	Action	Mon., 11:00 a.m.	Get Tommy down for morning nap on time. Let Mark know I will not be available from 11:00 a.m. to 12:00 p.m.

Task	Type	Time	Notes
Distribute contact list door-to-door with Tommy and Amy	Action	Sun., 10:00 a.m.	
Send mail testing interest in a block party	Action	Tues., 10:00 a.m.	
Research local weekend getaway options as surprise for Amy	Action	Wed., 11:00 a.m.	Get Tommy down for morning nap on time. Let Mark know I will not be available from 11:00 a.m. to 12:00 p.m.
Ask my parents if they can babysit the weekend we go away	Action	Wed., 11:00 a.m.	
Create a special e-mail address that only Amy and I will use to communicate	Action	Thurs., 11:00 a.m.	Get Tommy down for morning nap on time. Let Mark know I will not be available from 11:00 a.m. to 12:00 p.m.
Enroll Tommy in child-care center	Action	Fri., 10:00 a.m.	Let Mark know I will not be available from 10:00 a.m. to 11:00 a.m.

After Pete listed his Tweaks of the Week in his *Tweak It* worksheet, he put the activities in his *Tweak It* snapshot calendar and priority list :

Pete's *Tweak It* Snapshot Calendar and Priority List—Week 3

Monday	Tuesday	Wednesday	Thursday	Friday	Saturday	Sunday
Work whenever: 2:00 p.m. to 6:00 p.m.; 8:30 p.m. to 12:00 a.m.	Work whenever: 2:00 p.m. to 6:00 p.m.; 8:00 p.m. to 12:00 a.m.	Work whenever: 2:00 p.m. to 6:00 p.m.; 8:00 p.m. to 12:00 a.m.	Work whenever: 2:00 p.m. to 6:00 p.m.; 8:00 p.m. to 12:00 a.m.	Work whenever: 2:00 p.m. to 6:00 p.m.	Work whenever: 10:00 a.m. to 1:00 p.m.; 3:00 p.m. to 6:00 p.m.	Tech-free Sunday
7:00 a.m.: Wake up 7:30 a.m.: D-E-W routine 8:30 a.m.: Jog with stroller	7:00 a.m.: Wake up 7:30 a.m.: D-E-W routine	7:00 a.m.: Wake up 7:30 a.m.: D-E-W routine 8:30 a.m.: Jog with stroller	7:00 a.m.: Wake up 7:30 a.m.: D-E-W routine	7:00 a.m.: Wake up 7:30 a.m.: D-E-W routine 8:30 a.m.: Jog with stroller	Sleep in/Amy up with baby 7:30 a.m.: D-E-W routine	7:00 a.m.: Wake up 7:30 a.m.: D-E-W routine
11:00 a.m.: Create neighborhood contact list	10:00 a.m.: Send e-mail to list to offering to plan a block party and testing interest	11:00 a.m.: Research local weekend getaway options; ask parents to babysit	11:00 a.m.: Open special e-mail address for only me and Amy to use	11:00 a.m.: Enroll Tommy in child-care center	1:00 p.m.: Plan block party with Amy and three other neighbors who volunteered	10:00 a.m.: Distribute neighborhood contact list door-to-door with wife and Tommy
6:30 p.m.: Dinner 7:30 p.m.: In charge of bath/bedtime 10:00 p.m.: Pick Tweaks of the Week 12:00 a.m.: To bed	6:30 p.m.: Dinner and Triple S routine 12:00 a.m.: To bed	7:00 p.m.: Family dinner 8:00 p.m.: In charge of bath/bedtime 12:00 a.m.: To bed	6:30 p.m.: Dinner and Triple S routine 12:00 a.m.: To bed	6:30 p.m.: Dinner 7:30 p.m.: In charge of bath/bedtime 12:00 a.m.: To bed		5:30 p.m.: Family dinner and Triple S routine 11:00 p.m.: To bed

PETE'S TWEAKS OF THE WEEK—WEEK 4

By Tuesday, Amy and Pete got the hang of coordinating and trading off the evening household cleanup and bath/bedtime routines. Amy was thrilled when Pete told her about their long weekend away in a couple of months, and both he and Amy enjoyed the one or two messages they sent each other via the special e-mail box each day. Walking door-to-door with Tommy to deliver the neighborhood contact list was fun, and many people volunteered to help with the block party. Pete and Amy will start planning the party next month once he's settled into his new work schedule.

This week Pete's limited his unique tweaks to focus primarily on transitioning Tommy into his new routine at the child-care center. This is going to be a big adjustment for both Tommy and Pete. He's going to use his extra time to start networking locally and online. Pete wants to connect with the local entrepreneurs group. He's going to volunteer to handle communications for an upcoming summit they're hosting. He plans to ask a colleague he knows who's a member of the group out for lunch or coffee, and he will attend the group's weekly planning meeting. If he has time, he'll write a post for the blog he hasn't touched in a year.

He and Mark plan to map out how they want to coordinate their work now that Pete's schedule is less flexible but provides longer periods of overlapping availability. To break his habit of working "whenever and wherever," Pete will try to answer e-mails only three times a day and put his mobile phone in the trunk whenever he drives somewhere so he's not tempted to check it at every red light.

Pete's Tweak It Worksheet—Week 4

Standard Tweaks	Action or Priority	Target Date/Time	Communicate/Coordinate Plan
Pick Tweaks of the Week	Action	Mon., 10:00 p.m.	Confirm with Mark no calls with overseas customers/suppliers after 10:00 p.m. on Monday
Jog with Tommy in the stroller for thirty minutes three times a week	Action	Mon., 4:00 p.m.; Wed., 5:30 p.m.; Sat., 10:00 a.m.	Let Mark know I won't be able to respond to e-mails/have meetings from 4:00 p.m. to 5:00 p.m. on Monday and 5:30 p.m. to 6:30 p.m. on Wednesday.
Have a tech-free Sunday	Action	Sun.	Answer pending, urgent e-mails Saturday
Have family dinner together twice a week	Action	Wed., 7 p.m.; Sun., 5:30 p.m.	On weekday, make sure any meeting/call ends an hour before dinner; have Amy put the dates and times on her calendar as well
Coordinate Triple S and evening bath/bedtime routine coverage with Amy	Action	Mon., Tues., Fri.: cover bath/bedtime; and Wed., Thurs., Sun.: cover Triple S	Coordinate preferred nights with Amy on Sunday
D-E-W morning routine	Action	Mon.–Sun., 7:00 a.m. or 7:30 a.m.	Even though I will be tempted to check if there are e-mails from Mark, do this routine first, then check

Unique Tweaks of the Week	Action or Priority	Target Date/Time	Communicate/Coordinate Plan
Transition Tommy to start at child-care center	Action	Mon.–Fri., 8:00 a.m.	Leave Monday morning open
Meet with Mark to discuss revised work-flow coordination	Action	Tues., 9:00 a.m.	Send e-mail to Mark outlining new schedule on Monday
Practice responding to e-mails only three times a day twice a week	Priority		Confirm which times are the best with Mark and come up with a plan for how to reach you with an urgent issue
Put my mobile device in the trunk when driving	Priority		Put Post-it note on keys to remind me
Volunteer to handle the publicity and social media outreach for the upcoming local entrepreneurship summit	Action	Mon., 1:00 p.m.	
Schedule coffee or lunch with colleague	Action	Tues., 3:00 p.m.	
Write a post for my blog and send to five contacts who might be particularly interested in it	Action	Wed., 12:00 p.m.	Outline ideas for post earlier in the week
Attend entrepreneur summit planning meeting	Action	Fri., 11:00 a.m.	Let Mark know I will not be available between 11:00 a.m. and 1:00 p.m.

Once Pete had identified the small activities and priorities he wanted to focus on for the next seven days, he input them into his *Tweak It* snapshot calendar and priority list:

Pete's Tweak It Snapshot Calendar and Priority List—Week 4

Monday	Tuesday	Wednesday	Thursday	Friday	Saturday	Sunday
Work: 9:00 a.m. to 1:00 p.m.; 8:00 p.m. to 10:00 p.m.	Work: 9:00 a.m. to 3:00 p.m.; 8:00 p.m. to 10:00 p.m.	Work: 9:00 a.m. to 5:00 p.m.; 8:00 p.m. to 10:00 p.m.	Work: 9:00 a.m. to 4:00 p.m.; 8:00 p.m. to 10:00 p.m.	Work: 9:00 a.m. to 5:00 p.m.; 8:00 p.m. to 10:00 p.m.	Work: 1:00 p.m. to 3:00 p.m.	Tech-free Sunday
6:00 a.m.: Wake up 7:00 a.m.: D-E-W routine 8:00 a.m.: Drop off Tommy at center	6:00 a.m.: Wake up 7:00 a.m.: D-E-W routine 8:00 a.m.: Drop off Tommy at center	6:00 a.m.: Wake up 7:00 a.m.: D-E-W routine 8:00 a.m.: Drop off Tommy at center	6:00 a.m.: Wake up 7:00 a.m.: D-E-W routine 8:00 a.m.: Drop off Tommy at center	6:00 a.m.: Wake up 7:00 a.m.: D-E-W routine 8:00 a.m.: Drop off Tommy at center	Sleep in/Wife up with baby 7:30 a.m.: D-E-W routine	7:00 a.m.: Wake up 7:30 a.m.: D-E-W routine
1:00 p.m.: Volunteer for local entrepreneur summit	9:00 a.m.: Meet with Mark to discuss new schedule 3:00 p.m.: Schedule call with former colleague to catch up	12:00 p.m.: Write blog post; send to five contacts with note	3:00 p.m.: Talk to and catch up with former colleague	11:00 a.m.: Attend entrepreneur summit planning meeting	10:00 a.m.: Jog with Tommy in stroller	10:00 a.m.: Distribute neighborhood contact list door-to-door with wife and Tommy
1:30 p.m.: Pick Tommy up at center 4:00 p.m.: Jog with Tommy in stroller 6:30 p.m.: Dinner 7:30 p.m.: In charge of bath/bedtime 10:00 p.m.: Pick Tweaks of the Week 11:00 p.m.: To bed	3:30 p.m.: Pick Tommy up at center 6:30 p.m.: Dinner 7:30 p.m.: In charge of bath/bedtime 11:00 p.m.: To bed	5:30 a.m.: Pick Tommy up at center 7:00 p.m.: Family dinner and Triple S routine 11:00 p.m.: To bed	4:30 p.m.: Pick Tommy up at center 5:30 p.m.: Jog with Tommy in stroller 6:30 p.m.: Dinner and Triple S routine 11:00 p.m.: To bed	5:30 p.m.: Pick Tommy up at center 6:30 p.m.: Dinner 7:30 p.m.: In charge of bath/bedtime 11:00 p.m.: To bed		5:30 p.m.: Family dinner and Triple S routine 11:00 p.m.: To bed

Priority List

✓ Practice responding to and sending e-mails only three times a day
✓ Put your mobile device in the trunk when driving

Phase 3: Review and Revise

For the most part, Pete achieved his goal of putting more structure around the extreme flexibility in his work and life with the *Tweak It* practice. Tommy is in child care full-time, and having a morning and evening household routine in place means more is getting done at work and at home. Pete feels more connected to his wife and community.

But the "work whenever and wherever" mentality is hard to break. Even Pete was surprised by how much more he's able to get done now that he has eight unbroken hours to concentrate on work; however, it's hard not to check e-mails "one last time" at night, which is why he still ends up working evenings from 8 to 10 p.m. He's decided it's okay most nights, but he still wants to work on carving out more time for other things that matter to him. He was worried how clients would respond to his new, less flexible schedule, but there have been no problems.

TWEAK IT *SNAPSHOT CALENDAR AND PRIORITY LIST*:

No changes.

TWEAK IT *DEFINITION OF SUCCESS:*

Pete wants to strengthen the boundaries he's started to build around his work so that he can spend even more time with his son on the weekends and with his wife in the evenings.

STANDARD TWEAKS:

He's going to officially add "Check e-mails only three times a day" and "Put mobile phone in the trunk when I drive somewhere" to his list of standard tweaks, because taking those steps has helped him pay more attention throughout the day to what he is doing at the moment. Being less distracted, especially when he's with his family, feels great.

Tweak It *Practice Stories Summary:*

Lisa, Jeff, Denise, and Pete are four people with very different priorities and activities that matter to them right now. But the consistent use of the *Tweak It* practice helped each of them build a more solid foundation of well-being and order, one small step at a time.

What's Next:

How have the *Tweak It* Practice Stories motivated you to get in better shape, eat better food, get a handle on your personal finances, learn a new job skill, or work on your professional network? Don't get stuck on the question, Where do I begin? In the following *Tweak It* Inspiration section, more than fifty experts will share their simplest tips to get you started. There's no excuse for not moving forward with your own *Tweak It* practice!

TWEAK IT
INSPIRATION

TWEAK IT INSPIRATION: AN OVERVIEW

When I started to share the *Tweak It* practice, people would get very excited and say, "I want to start to be more involved in my community," "I want to organize my house," and "I want to learn about technology!" But then almost as quickly they'd throw up their hands in defeat and wonder, "But where do I begin?" The lack of small, concrete, get-started steps caused them to lose momentum.

To help people avoid this roadblock and continue to move forward, I began to keep track of the most common areas people told me they wanted to focus on as part of their *Tweak It* practice. Then I found experts who specialized in each area, and asked them to share their very best, simplest get-started wisdom. The results are the small, concrete *Tweak It* Inspiration tips that you will find in this section of the book in the following areas:

Renew Tweaks
- ✓ Move Your Body
- ✓ Choose Healthy Food
- ✓ Prepare Healthy Meals
- ✓ Get More Sleep
- ✓ Learn to Meditate
- ✓ Do Nothing...Often
- ✓ Take a Vacation
- ✓ Celebrate Good Times
- ✓ Create, Dream, Escape
- ✓ Practice Your Faith
- ✓ Give Something Back
- ✓ Manage Tech Distraction

Career Tweaks
- ✓ Build Your Network
- ✓ Create Virtual You
- ✓ Update Your Skills
- ✓ Learn New Technologies
- ✓ Know Your "Type"
- ✓ For Younger Workers
- ✓ For Older Workers
- ✓ Plan a Career Break
- ✓ Find an Encore (Preretirement) Career
- ✓ Start Your Own Business

Money Tweaks
- ✓ Everyday Finances
- ✓ Retirement Savings
- ✓ College Savings

Connect Tweaks
- ✓ Loved Ones
- ✓ Friends
- ✓ Date
- ✓ Community

Connect with Kids Tweaks
- ✓ Kids under Thirteen Years
- ✓ Teens
- ✓ Just for Dads
- ✓ Nieces/Nephews
- ✓ Technology
- ✓ School
- ✓ College Planning
- ✓ SAT Prep

Caregiving Tweaks
- ✓ Elder Care—General
- ✓ Elder Care—with Siblings
- ✓ Child Care—Regular and Backup
- ✓ Summer Care

Maintenance Tweaks
- ✓ Your Health
- ✓ Your Personal Appearance
- ✓ Your Car
- ✓ Your House—Get Organized
- ✓ Your House—Clean It Yourself
- ✓ Your House—Hire Cleaning Help
- ✓ Your House—Maintain It

I've known many of the experts I interviewed for years, and I am excited to share their knowledge with you. Other experts were recommended highly by people I admire, and after speaking with them I, too, have become a fan, and so will you. What all the experts have in common is a passionate commitment to serve and help others. Evidence of that commitment is the active and robust online presence all the experts maintain that will allow you to connect with and continue to learn from them once you've mastered their get-started advice. You can access the knowledge of these fifty-plus experts three ways:

- Read their get-started tweaks previewed in this section of the book.
- Check out the additional and more detailed tweaks and stories in the *Tweak It* online community (www.tweakittogether.com).
- Connect with each expert directly via the link provided.

Each page in this section contains "tweak" advice from a different expert. Let's begin with the small activities and priorities that will help you to renew your mind, body, and soul in our modern, hectic world.

Chapter 11

Renew Tweaks

Quite simply, we don't take care of ourselves physically, mentally, and emotionally. The data tell the story:

- Seventy percent of men and women are considered overweight or obese.[1]
- Twenty-five percent of Americans take some type of medication every year to help them sleep.[2]
- Eighteen percent of the population has some type of anxiety disorder, and doctors wrote 46.3 million prescriptions for antianxiety drugs in 2010 (*New York Times*).[3]
- Forty-six percent of "wired and ready" workers say that the Internet, e-mail, cell phones, and instant messaging have increased their level of stress.[4]
- Fifty-seven percent of working Americans have unused vacation time at the end of the year.[5]

The commitment to renew and care for "you" must be an ongoing priority, especially today. You must take charge of defining where work time ends and me time begins. It doesn't mean you have to be model-thin, run a marathon, follow a vegan diet, take a month off, or join a meditation ashram. As the following experts explain in this chapter, very simple activities and priorities that you can easily make part of your weekly *Tweak It* routine will have a big impact on your overall sense of health and well-being:

- **Move Your Body:** Pamela Peeke (www.drpeeke.com), MD, MPH, FACP, author of *Fight Fat after Forty* and the author of the blog "Everyday Fitness with Pamela Peeke" on WebMD.com

- **Choose Healthy Food:** Marissa Lippert, author of *The Cheater's Diet* and founder of Nourish, a nutrition counseling and communications firm in New York City (http://nourish-nyc.com/)

- **Prepare Healthy Meals:** Aviva Goldfarb, author of *SOS! The Six O'Clock Scramble to the Rescue: Earth-Friendly, Kid-Pleasing Dinners for Busy Families* (www.thescramble.com)

- **Get More Sleep:** Ben Rubin, cofounder of Zeo, Inc. (www.myzeo .com), a company dedicated to help people take control of their sleep

- **Learn to Meditate:** Judy Martin (www.worklifenation.com), meditation and relaxation expert and creator of Practical Chaos™, a practical meditation program for busy professionals

- **Do Nothing:** Karen Salmansohn (www.notsalmon.com), a graphic artist and bestselling author who has sold more than 1 million books, including *How to Be Happy, Dammit* and *The Bounce Back Book*

- **Take a Vacation:** Matt Villano, veteran travel journalist and blogger of *Adventures with Matt* for the U.S. Travel Association's website (insiders.seeamerica.com/insiders/american_outdoors_insider)

- **Celebrate Good Times:** Elizabeth Mascali, coauthor of *Plan to Party* and cofounder of Party Bluprints, Inc. (www.partybluprintsblog.com)

- **Create, Dream, Escape:** Julie Burstein (www.pursuitofspark.com), author of *Spark* and former producer of Public Radio International's *Studio 360*; Whitney Johnson (www.whitneyjohnson.com), venture capitalist, *Harvard Business Review* blogger, and author of *Dare, Dream, Do*; Sarah Robinson, community developer and creator of the blog *Escaping Mediocrity* (www.escaping-mediocrity.com)
- **Practice Your Faith:** Rick Hamlin, executive editor of *Guideposts* magazine (www.Guideposts.org) and author of the blog *On the Journey*
- **Give Something Back:** Sloane Berrent, founder of thecausemopoli tan.com, which to date has raised over $2.5 million for nonprofits
- **Manage Tech Distraction:** Maggie Jackson (www.maggie-jackson .com), award-winning author of *Distracted: The Erosion of Attention and the Coming Dark Age*

Move your body

WHY IS IT IMPORTANT TO MOVE YOUR BODY?

Just get up and assume the vertical more often. It's important for both the mind and body. People only think of benefits for the body but they are actually missing the fact that the mind is part of the body. When you do physical activity, you actually build, refresh, and rejuvenate the neuronal circuits in your brain. This helps you learn things better and hold on to that information. It gives you a crisp memory and decreases dementia.

—Pamela Peeke, MD, MPH, FACP

Tweak: It's very important that physical activity becomes integral to your life. It's not negotiable. You know you have to just get off the couch and move more. Educate yourself.

Tweak: Increase your activity of daily living. How about cleaning up that closet, or the garage? How about decluttering your kitchen or your bedroom? How about cleaning up those cabinets in your bathroom and other places you swore you would do five years ago? The more you declutter the better you feel about yourself, and you will be burning calories right and left.

Tweak: Put the headset on, and stand up and walk while you are on the phone. You've got to talk on the telephone at work, but that's why God made headsets, right? Just walk, pace, and talk all day long.

Tweak: Time your sitting. For every hour you have to sit, count on five to ten minutes where you get up and move. Add a minute here, a minute there. Five hours of sitting equals twenty-five to fifty minutes of movement.

For more tweaks and resources, go to www.tweakittogether.com/move yourbody.

Make healthy food choices

WHY IS IT IMPORTANT TO MAKE HEALTHY FOOD CHOICES?

Bottom line, making healthy food choices is about energy and efficiency. With your body, food comes first. Think of your body like a car. If you're not fueling it, it can't operate well and it's going to sputter out after a short period of time. People always complain about the crash and burn at three or four o'clock. They're running for coffee or chocolate or sweets. They're crashing because either they haven't fueled themselves well enough earlier in the day or they're not providing themselves with another little shot of good nutritious fuel when they need it.

—Marissa Lippert

Tweak: Do not skip meals. Eat every three to four hours. Continue to stoke the fire, or the flames will go out. We need to eat to keep our energy levels high throughout the day. Eat moderate portions. The more nutrient-dense and wholesome a meal or snack is, the less you need to fill up.

Tweak: Make grocery shopping an appointment on your weekly calendar. Go on a certain day at least once a week. Once you are at the store, do the following: **(1) Shop the perimeter first.** That should be where most of your food comes from. The inner aisles are where the processed, packaged foods—the less healthy kind—are found. **(2) Look at the ingredients lists on packaged foods. If there are more than three to five items that you cannot pronounce or that you've never heard of before, leave the box on the shelf.** The fewer ingredients and the less processed packaged food you buy, the better.

Tweak: Allow yourself to indulge sometimes. There's no need to cut out things that you enjoy. Usually I encourage people to aim for two more indulgent or fun meals a week and two really good desserts. That gives them structure within a typical week.

For more tweaks and resources, go to www.tweakittogether.com/healthy foodchoices.

Prepare healthy meals

WHY IS IT IMPORTANT TO PREPARE HEALTHY MEALS?

The way we eat can really affect our stress level, our budget and our health. What most people do is stand in front of the refrigerator at six o'clock and say, "What am I going to make for dinner?" which is a completely stressful and exhausting event at the end of the day or after work. People have told me this over and over again that once you have a plan and have all the ingredients making dinner is no big deal. You'll actually enjoy the process. It can truly be life changing. Not only that, but you will find that planning meals can be a big money saver.

—Aviva Goldfarb

Tweak: Once a week, sit down with your recipes and your calendar, and pick the recipes you're going to make for the week. Mark them or set them aside somewhere so that you can easily access them during the week.

Tweak: Make a grocery list based on the recipes you've chosen. Don't forget to include simple side dishes. Then add to the list whatever other items you need to get through the whole week so you won't have to shop twice or more that week.

Tweak: Pull out the recipe each morning that you're going make so that when you get home from work you will be ready to go. What's so time-consuming and stressful is trying to figure out what to make. You've already done that, which is very efficient. Now the family member who gets home first, even if it's before you, can get the recipe started.

Tweak: After you've enjoyed a meal, make any notes on the recipe for what you would do differently. If your family didn't love the recipe, toss it. Then make a file of your favorite recipes so that when you plan meals in the future weeks it's easy. On my site, Six O' Clock Scramble, you can do this by saving your favorites.

For more tweaks and resources, go to www.tweakittogether.com/prepare healthymeals.

Get more sleep

WHY IS IT IMPORTANT TO GET MORE AND BETTER SLEEP?

Sleep is as important as diet or exercise in your life. We sleep a third of our time on the planet. It's highly restorative for your body and your mind, yet people don't pay as much attention to sleep as they do other areas of their health and wellness. It's viewed as a natural right and something that we shouldn't have to work on. As a result, many of us aren't optimizing the quality of our work and the quality of our life because we short-change our sleep.

—Ben Rubin

Tweak: Get your personal sleep data. If you don't measure it, you're not going to manage it. Having data on how you sleep allows you to create a feedback loop. At the very basic level, you can just use a sleep journal. At Zeo, we provide tools that enable you to measure your sleep. We offer free iOS and Android apps that help you measure your sleep using your cell phone.

Tweak: Reset your midnight, or sync your body with the sun. In the morning, get bright light exposure between an hour and two hours after you get up. Go outside and take a walk to get about twenty to thirty minutes of good light exposure. The other alternative is to use a blue light or a white light, like the Phillips goLite BLU. Press a button every morning and it gives you twenty minutes of bright light.

Tweak: Limit light exposure at night. Reduce light exposure at night when you're not supposed to be getting it. Simply use dimmer lights inside and don't sit in front of the computer late at night. If you're going to sit in front of a computer late at night, use a program like f.lux (stereopsis.com/flux/) that filters out the light exposure that can shift your circadian rhythm. Another option is to use blue-blocking sunglasses, which are basically an orange pair of shades. Pop those on at 8 p.m. and use them until you go to bed.

For more tweaks and resources, go to www.tweakittogether.com/get moresleep.

Meditate for mindfulness

WHY IS IT IMPORTANT TO PRACTICE MINDFUL MEDITATION?

Meditation is about controlling our brain waves. No matter where we go and what we do, we're in a state of peace. The bottom line is that if we're in a peaceful state, no matter what comes at us, we're going to respond from a place of wisdom instead of from a place of fear. We can control all the chatter that goes on in the mind with meditation.

—Judy Martin

Tweak: When you wake up in the morning, be aware of your breath. Have a little sign next to your bed as a reminder. On awakening, take a couple of deep breaths—not just shallow breaths into your chest, but into your diaphragm. That immediately wakes you up, but it also keeps you in a state of calm. Experiment with how that feels for two to three minutes.

Tweak: Place the word *Breathe* on a Post-it at work to remind you to stop and breathe in and out for three minutes. When you take a breath before a busy project or something you have to really focus on, it stimulates the front of the brain, which calms you down and makes you more creative. Some people have their iPhones go off every hour as a reminder to take five minutes and just pay attention to the ins and the outs of their breathing. It will have a physiological impact on the body and the central nervous system, as it triggers the parasympathetic nervous system, which creates a calm or relaxed state. Researchers call this the relaxation response.

Tweak: Pick a relaxing place at home. Find a quiet, low-light place in your home. Engage your senses. Smell. Sight. Hearing. Touch. Lower the light and the sensory overload. Close the door and maybe play some light music in the background. Put a little bit of lavender oil on your wrist if you're not allergic to it, or close the door to the bathroom and put some in the bathtub, run the hot water, and steam up the bathroom. That will calm you down in three seconds. If you have a walk-in closet, try that for a quiet space. Use what you have available to you.

For more tweaks and resources, go to www.tweakittogether.com/practice mindfulness.

Do nothing

—Karen Salmansohn

For more tweaks and resources, go to www.tweakittogether.com/donothing.

Take a vacation

WHY IS IT IMPORTANT TO TAKE A VACATION?

According to a recent Harris Interactive study conducted on behalf of JetBlue, nearly 70 percent of respondents will leave an average of eleven days of unused vacation on the table this year. If the average American is leaving eleven vacation days on the table, almost everyone can benefit from taking these steps toward building in some time to decompress.

—Matt Villano

Tweak: Create a travel fund. Transfer $50 or $100 from your main account into a separate savings account that you label "travel." Setting up this travel fund makes travel viable for everyone regardless of income. Then it's up to you to make sure that you're spending within your means when you go away. It helps you to budget a trip and figure out exactly what you can afford.

Tweak: Set up a dream box. This can be a box or a file. For us, it's a wonderful clay-fired ceramic jar that we got in Peru. If you read something in a magazine about a place that you think sounds interesting, clip it out and put it in the box. If you are watching a TV show and you see Matt Lauer visiting someplace that looks beautiful, write it down on a piece of paper and put it in the dream box. The dream box is a place for you to store viable options for your next vacation. Go through every year and edit the box. Pick a trip that's realistic now and start planning. (Another option is to create an online folder at Evernote.com.)

Tweak: Read about travel for inspiration. The best way to expand your horizons and knowledge is to read about places you can travel to. Feature articles that go in depth can introduce you to a particular place that you may have never even considered visiting.

Tweak: At least one day a month, get out of the house. At least once a month, you should actively seek adventure and new experience in your immediate world. Leave before breakfast and come home when it's dark. Go to your nearest metro area or national park.

For more tweaks and resources, go to www.tweakittogether.com/takea vacation.

Celebrate good times

WHY IS IT IMPORTANT TO CELEBRATE GOOD TIMES?

Parties are a perfect opportunity for you to connect with the people in your life. Find a way to entertain from your heart, not because you have to or you should, but because it's a gift that you want to give. There's nothing better than that. There's no perfect way to entertain. There's no set formula. Just understand why you're doing it, which is to create and share an experience with people in your life.

—Elizabeth Mascali

Tweak: Start with a small celebration. If you are overwhelmed, keep it small. Let it be intimate. Do it on your terms—what feels good for you, what fits into your schedule—whether it's a glass of wine and cheese, a cup of tea, or a breakfast.

Tweak: Invite your guests. This sounds easy, but a lot of people struggle with "If I invite so-and-so from the neighborhood, then I have to invite these three other people from the neighborhood." If you plan a party once every six weeks, once every eight weeks, or every quarter, you'll ultimately get to them all. You have to be okay with not being able to invite everybody at the same time.

Tweak: Break out what you're going to need to do for your party. Decide up front. If you look at our book, we do this with our detailed party plans. People have very good intentions when they put the date on the calendar and send out the invites, but then all of a sudden life happens. It's the day before the party and they're running out to the store trying to do everything all at once. That's not a positive experience. Having a plan and lists allows you to look at the concrete tasks that have to get done by what date. It makes you feel empowered: "I can manage it."

Tweak: Personalize your party. Put a few special touches on your gathering that will make your guests think, *Wow, they really took time, thought ahead, planned, and they did this nice little thing for me.* Whether it's a favor, a personalized name card at the table, or the music playlist that went along with the party, these efforts make it all very personal and enhance the experience.

For more tweaks and resources, go to www.tweakittogether.com/celebrate goodtimes.

Create, dream, escape

A recent segment on NPR's *All Things Considered* featured the story of Toni Messina, a fifty-year-old suburban mom and lawyer who also loves to dance flamenco. "Flamenco's got attitude. It makes me feel like I've got attitude." The story chronicled Messina's search for flamenco's duende, or "a magical moment of abandon." Journeying all the way to Jerez, Spain, the birthplace of the dance, she got close enough to the duende experience that, she recalled, "tears filled my eyes." Think about how much more full and vibrant your work and life would be if you experienced a little more duende and were able to create, dream, and escape, too.

WHY IS IMPORTANT TO CREATE?

> Creativity is a part of our everyday lives whether we like it or not. If we're conscious about it, we can open up new paths to creativity in all the areas that require us to offer fresh ideas. It's satisfying to make something out of nothing (even if it's not perfect!).
>
> —Julie Burstein

Tweak: Create a process that will help you continue forward. The artist Chuck Close says that when you want to make something new, keep at it and create a process that helps you. Continue to work even when it's hard. That's what will get you to something new. For me, the process I created was to make myself just sit down and crochet in the playroom whenever we gathered as a family to watch TV.

Tweak: Make mistakes and leave room for change. When you make a mistake, learn from it and use it to create something even more powerful or beautiful. Don't give in to the despair (or maybe give in a little bit), then take what you've learned and say, "What if I tried this?" Mistakes can lead to something really cool you've never thought of before.

WHY IS IT IMPORTANT TO DREAM?

We dream to make meaning of our lives, to truly grow up, and to show our children how to dream. Dreaming is about finding our voice. What do I want to stand for? What's my legacy going to be in my life?

—Whitney Johnson

Tweak: Observe whom you admire and respect and why. It's likely that they're doing something or behaving in a way that's actually a piece of you. They're mirroring for you who you are. That's going to help you see yourself out in the bigger world, and you can start to see the possibilities.

Tweak: Throughout the day, balance your Batman and Robin moments. We dream best when we not only dream for ourselves but help other people dream. When we're Batman we're dreaming for ourselves, and when we're Robin we're helping other people dream. We need to be both.

WHY IS IT IMPORTANT TO ESCAPE?

We're supposed to have moments of amazement regularly. If we are trapped in the hamster wheel of mediocre living and feeling like everything we do is drudgery, then we're missing out, and the people who love us are missing out because we are absolutely not our best selves.

—Sarah Robinson

Tweak: Take a different route to work. Leave a few minutes early and take a different route or different type of transportation. You will be forced to respond differently and you will see new things. You won't be on autopilot.

Tweak: Don't do what you usually do for lunch. If you usually bring
   lunch, don't bring lunch. If you usually don't bring lunch, bring lunch
   because it's different. The whole point is to get us out of the autopilot
   patterns that make life feel like drudgery.

For more tweaks and resources, go to www.tweakittogether.com/create
dreamescape.

Practice your faith

WHY IS IT IMPORTANT TO PRACTICE YOUR FAITH?

One of the biggest problems we all face in life is keeping a perspective, seeing things from the bird's-eye view. It's hard to remember
what's important and what doesn't deserve as much anxiety or
worry. Following a spiritual practice keeps pulling you back to the
larger picture.

—Rick Hamlin

Tweak: Pick a time and place to practice your faith. Five minutes
   of truly being silent, focusing, and meditating has a huge value. A practice that's once a week for twenty-five minutes is not nearly as valuable
   as one you do five times a week for five minutes. For over twenty years,
   I've used my commute to meditate and pray.
Tweak: Pray through a prayer list. I give myself about thirty names.
   Be intentional. Instead of reading the list, let your mind do the work
   as you pray, and let go. It's also important when we're praying for others to pray for our own family and to acknowledge our own needs
   because they are going to come up into the silence. If you have anxiety,
   don't edit yourself, because that stifles prayer.
Tweak: Try zapping and waiting prayers. Long ago a friend who is a Hol-
   lywood producer told me about zapping prayers. In our work life, when

somebody gets agitated, zap that person with a silent affirmation, encouragement, patience, or understanding. Also, there are so many times you end up having to wait. Think about the times when you put in a Google search and then you have to wait for the results. Instead of using those waits to get anxious or impatient, use that waiting time to pray.

Tweak: Post or answer a prayer on social media. There are real spiritual communities on Twitter and Facebook. Depending on your workload, post a prayer request or respond to a prayer request. We have our prayer website at www.Guideposts.org.

For more tweaks and resources, go to www.tweakittogether.com/practice faith.

Give something back

WHY IS IT IMPORTANT TO GIVE SOMETHING BACK?

Feel empowered for what you *can* do instead of guilty for what you can't do. People will always wish they could give more time, money, and services. Everyone wants to do more, but it's important to just be active. The fact that you want to give, do the research, or take any of the steps I'm going to share is great. If life gets busy and hectic, that's okay because you've done part of the work. Give yourself permission to go back and continue later when you can.

—Sloane Berrent

Tweak: Figure out areas you are passionate about. Get a piece of paper and a pen—don't go in front of the computer, don't go in front of your phone. Sit down with the white piece of paper and write down what causes you are passionate about and would be valuable for you.

Tweak: Stick your toe in the water and try a cause. Try one or more causes out to see how they resonate. Do you like their messaging? Do you feel they're giving you the right kinds of information? Don't go crazy and bequeath your entire wealth. Don't commit yourself to volunteer or do pro bono work every weekend for the next year. You're testing it out. Allow yourself to determine if you think they're doing the right thing. If they are, then get a little bit more involved.

Tweak: Give back and have fun. Get a couple of friends together and visit a soup kitchen. Maybe your alumni association has a volunteer day. Don't feel you have to plan everything yourself. There are lots of organizations out there that preplan volunteer events. Get a couple of your friends, take your family and your coworkers, or have your company sponsor coworkers to participate in a breast cancer walk or something similar.

For more tweaks and resources, go to www.tweakittogether.com/giveback.

Manage tech distraction

WHY IS IT IMPORTANT TO MANAGE TECH DISTRACTION?

We don't realize that the pace and speed of the technology is instant: push-button, point-and-click. Inevitably, it makes us forget the idea of slow incubation, of the percolation of ideas, of hanging in the moment of uncertainty and frustration that's an important part of learning. We have to remind ourselves, our kids, and the people who work with us that slow is okay and beneficial. You can have the brief, faceless communication of technology, but you also really need to have the rich, face-to-face, multilayered communication moments in every area of your life.

—Maggie Jackson

Tweak: Create boundaries around technology with the clock.
Using the boundaries of the clock, especially in a 24/7 society, is an

underutilized tool for managing distraction. It sounds simple, but I don't think people do it enough. When you're on vacation, think, *I'll check in with work from 9 to 10 a.m. in the morning and let everybody know that.* Or *I'm going to be with my family from 6 to 9 p.m.*

Tweak: Tinker with not responding to technology immediately. Be proactive, not reactive. People allow communications to rule *them* when they're always answering e-mails, rather than shaping the course of their day and setting aside a specific time for answering e-mail. If you're reacting all day long, you're not utilizing what's called executive attention, which is the skill set of planning and analysis.

Tweak: Pick one conversation during the week and experiment with giving the gift of your full attention. The gift of attention takes three parts: (1) put the hardware out of reach, (2) turn your eyes away from the screen, and (3) put your mind into the conversation. It's environmental, it's physical, and it's cognitive.

For more tweaks and resources, go to www.tweakittogether.com/tech distraction.

Chapter 12

Career Tweaks

For me, the most lasting images of the Great Recession were the people I met who seemed to be caught off guard professionally and found their jobs and careers vulnerable. They hadn't built a solid professional network. They didn't have an online professional presence. Their skills were out of date. They were unfamiliar and uncomfortable with new technologies, and they didn't have any insights into how they preferred to work that they could leverage into a new job or career.

Then there were those who had made more major career transitions without giving them enough advance thought. They took a career break and were struggling to get back into the workforce. They'd retired early into another career that wasn't what they'd expected, or they started their own business only to realize entrepreneurship wasn't for them.

In all cases, the common refrain was "I didn't know what to do, and I didn't have time." The experts in this chapter will share simple activities and priorities to make the ongoing, active, thoughtful management of your career part of your weekly *Tweak It* routine so that no one is caught off guard again:

- **Build Your Network:** Michael Melcher (www.michaelmelcher .com), career coach and author of *The Creative Lawyer: A Practical Guide to Authentic Professional Satisfaction*
- **Create Virtual You:** Miriam Salpeter (www.KeppieCareers.com), author of *Social Networking for Career Success* and career blogger for USNews.com
- **Update Your Skills:** Alexandra Levit (www.alexandralevit.com), career expert and author of *Blind Spots: The 10 Business Myths You Can't Afford to Believe on Your New Path to Success.*
- **Learn New Technologies:** Carley Knobloch, Founder of Digitwirl, a web show making tech actually work for you (www.digitwirl.com)
- **Know Your "Type":** Susan Cain (www.thepowerofintroverts.com), Myers Briggs (MBTI) expert and author of *Quiet: The Power of Introverts in a World That Can't Stop Talking*
- **For Younger Workers:** Lindsey Pollak (www.lindseypollack.com), author of *Getting from College to Career: 90 Things to Do before You Join the Real World* and global spokesperson for LinkedIn.com
- **For Older Workers:** Phyllis Mufson, twenty-five-year career coach veteran and a top Twitter expert for job seekers (www.twitter.com/#!/ phyllismufson)
- **Plan a Career Break:** Carol Fishman Cohen, cofounder of iRelaunch, the return-to-work experts (www.iRelaunch.com), and author of *Back on the Career Track*
- **Find an Encore (Preretirement) Career:** Marci Alboher, author of *The Encore Career Handbook* (New York: Workman, 2013) and vice president of Civic Ventures (www.Encore.org)
- **Start Your Own Business:** Adelaide Lancaster, author of *The Big Enough Company* and founder of In Good Company, Inc. (www .ingoodcompany.com)

Build your network

WHY IS IT IMPORTANT TO BUILD YOUR NETWORK?

> Each person brings certain talents, energies, capabilities, and perspectives to their work. The way you get full value out of this is by connecting with people over time. It's really a lost opportunity not to do so. People are still the primary way that real information is transmitted. It's well established that many, if not most, job and business opportunities are not listed publicly but are shared person to person.
>
> —Michael Melcher

Tweak: Get together with one person each week. It could be a close friend or it could be a distant friend, but meet somebody for lunch, coffee, drinks, or dinner. If you connect with one person per week, you will have a pretty thriving network over time.

Tweak: Keep a simple log of whom you are reaching out to by phone or e-mail. It can be a spreadsheet or a bunch of scraps of paper in a box, as long as it keeps you aware of your progress. It's these simple habits, developed over time, that show results.

Tweak: Introduce people to each other. Think of all the people you know and who might like to meet each other. Who are two fun young people at the same point in their careers? Who are two working parents who have been managing child-care issues?

Tweak: Send interesting articles to people. This is really easy to do. All you have to say is, "Hey, Kim, I saw this article and thought of you, in case you haven't read it." A big part of networking is just reminding people you're around. In addition, it's a way to forge common connections.

Tweak: Volunteer for a task that will put you in the center of things. Be an alumni coordinator for your school. Help organize a conference or an annual event for a civic group. Any experience that gives you a specific function where you are interacting with other people is very useful for networking. It gives you a way to relate to people naturally, without having to come up with a networking agenda. This is particularly useful for people who may feel shy about networking.

For more tweaks and resources, go to www.tweakittogether.com/build network.

Create virtual you

WHY IS IT IMPORTANT TO CREATE VIRTUAL YOU?

There are four reasons why people should consider creating an online presence and why the skeptics shouldn't be so skeptical and dive in: (1) Social media is a great way to learn what thought leaders in your individual industry are thinking and writing about. When we're working and busy with our own lives, it's hard to keep up with what's new and what's hot in our field. (2) Social media is a helpful way to meet new people and expand your network exponentially beyond what you probably could do with your in-person connections. (3) Using social media helps demonstrate your expertise. Share with people what you know and show them how you can solve their problems. (4) Social media helps you be found. Anybody who is active online, expands his or her network, and demonstrates particular expertise is, in effect, posting a dynamic résumé online that employers have access to all the time.

—Miriam Salpeter

Tweak: Identify what you want to be known for and how that fits into what employers are looking for. What are people looking for when they're thinking of someone with your skill set? Find job descriptions that would interest you.

Tweak: Pull out key words to use in social media. What are the
words that came up over and over again in the job descriptions you
just searched for? Those are the words that you are going to use frequently throughout the social media profile you'll create.

Tweak: Set up a profile on LinkedIn. Set up a LinkedIn page and use
those key words on your list as you fill out your profile completely.

Tweak: Practice engaging with others in LinkedIn. Identify a couple
of groups to participate in to demonstrate your expertise and to connect with people. See what's going on in the group. What are people
talking about? If you can showcase your thoughts and suggestions,
then do it.

For more tweaks and resources, go to www.tweakittogether.com/virtualyou.

Update your skills

WHY IS IT IMPORTANT TO UPDATE YOUR SKILLS?

During the downturn, people were caught off guard because they
were stuck in the traditional way of working. You got your first job out
of school in a company and then let the tide carry you along. But no
one works that way anymore. All of us are going to have a series of different jobs in a series of different industries whether we like it or not.
That's just the way the tide is turning. And so you have to be thinking
one step ahead. Not just thinking how marketable I am today, but how
marketable I will be in five to ten years. And will the industry I am in
still be viable in this time frame? What's the next thing on the horizon
for me, whether it's a different position or a different industry?

—Alexandra Levit

Tweak: Check out the Bureau of Labor Statistics' *Occupational*
Outlook Handbook, **which is available at www.bls.gov/ooh.**
They have hundreds of thousands of occupations listed. Poke around.

What kind of education is required? What kind of skills are they asking for? Gradually start doing your homework.

Tweak: Figure out the skills you need to acquire. Now that you've identified industries and jobs, look at the skills you'd need. For example, "I'm entry-level right now, but I want to be in middle management. I see that communication, public-speaking skills, and problem-solving skills are perceived as important, so I'm going to take a course to hone those skills in preparation for the future."

Tweak: Take online classes to preview and test. Take an online course that is an hour or two long in the particular area you want to get more skilled in. Try a free webinar. For example, for technology skills go to a site like Lynda.com. There's no risk involved, and there's often no money involved. You can see how much getting that skill is going to cost and if it's worth it. It's important to do some up-front work, especially before you decide to quit everything to get an additional degree.

For more tweaks and resources, go to www.tweakittogether.com/update skills.

Learn new technologies

WHY IS IT IMPORTANT TO LEARN NEW TECHNOLOGIES?

Not learning and keeping up with new technology is like having an army of personal assistants waiting to help you and you're saying, "No thanks, I'm good." We all could use some help. All of these apps, web services, and gadgets act as additional brainpower, legwork, and manpower to help you run your life and your career. There's a big misconception that technology is for people who are technically inclined. But these applications are being designed now to work for everybody, even people who are not technically inclined, so there is almost no excuse not to learn them.

—Carley Knobloch

Tweak: Pick one technology, master it, and then move on. Go slow. Don't overwhelm yourself. You'll shut down and end up doing nothing. Don't get caught up in the whole "me too" syndrome, where you feel you have to become a member of that social network or install this app on your phone.

Tweak: Get help from online tutorials. When you're trying to adopt new technologies, YouTube is fantastic. Find a tutorial, a podcast, or even just an individual video.

Tweak: Subscribe to audio podcasts in areas that interest you. We may not have huge blocks of time where we can just relax with a good book. But we have ten minutes here, fifteen minutes there, and there are a lot of really great five-, ten-, or fifteen-minute podcasts where you can learn about world events, how to be better at your job, or even Impressionist art. Whatever your passion, give your brain a little break from whatever you're working on and tap into a different part of your intellect and your passion. I have certain food podcasts that I listen to every week. I never catch them on the radio when they're actually airing, but because I subscribe, I can listen to them at my leisure. It's fun and inspiring.

For more tweaks and resources, go to www.tweakittogether.com/learn newtech.

Know your "type"

WHY IS IT IMPORTANT TO KNOW YOUR "TYPE"?

Introversion and extroversion are at the heart of human nature. When you make life choices that match your temperament, you unleash amazing stores of energy. But when you spend time battling your own nature, the opposite happens and you're depleted. I've met so many people who live lives that don't suit them. For example, introverts who have crazy social schedules, or extroverts whose jobs require them to sit in front of their computers all day. Yes, we all have to do things that don't come naturally some of the time. That's part of growing and that's part of life, but if you find that you're spending too much of your social time or your work time living in ways that don't fit your type, then that's a clear signal that you need to make a change.

—Susan Cain

Tweak: Take the Myers Briggs test. There are all kinds of official resources you can use to take the test, but you can get the gist of the test in much simpler ways. First, there's a website called www.person alitypage.com where you can take a simplified version of the test. Once you get your results specifying which type you are, the authors walk you through what it means. Also, read the book *Do What You Are*, by Paul Tieger. It not only identifies your type, but it helps you think about what career changes you might need to make, and lets you celebrate that you're already in the right spot.

Tweak: Apply what you've learned about types to understand other people. When you meet people or think about people you know well, consider what their type might be. How is it different from yours, and how might that shape what they want from the world? How might your relationship work better?

Tweak: If you're an introvert, build in zones throughout the day to recharge.

Tweak: If you're an extrovert, make sure you get the social time that you need.

For more tweaks and resources, go to www.tweakittogether.com/know yourtype.

For younger workers

*WHY IS IT IMPORTANT FOR YOUNGER WORKERS TO TWEAK
THEIR CAREERS?*

> Gen-Ys/Millennials have seen their parents and neighbors laid off
> from jobs. They've seen a decrease in the number of companies
> recruiting on their college campuses. They are aware that you have
> to manage your career and that nobody else is going to do it for you.
> But rather than thinking only about their careers in the corporate
> world, they're also thinking about alternatives. Can I start my own
> business? Can I consult? Can I freelance? The idea that you shouldn't
> just have one way of earning a living seems to be very popular.
>
> —Lindsey Pollak

Tweak: Take a writing and public-speaking class. Written and verbal
communication is becoming a lost art. The young people who can write
well on e-mail and express themselves comfortably in person are going
to win. Listen to the Grammar Girl weekly podcast(www.grammar
.quickanddirtytips.com) Sign up for a business-writing class at a community college or online.

**Tweak: Check that your online image or professional brand is
consistent.** Make sure that if somebody Googles you they're going to
find impressive, professional information. Have a Google Alert on your
own name to make sure you're monitoring anything about yourself
that comes up. Update your résumé and LinkedIn profile frequently to
make sure that you're keeping your status updates current, and accept
connection requests. Have a really great photo that you select carefully. You never know who might be searching for you.

**Tweak: Keep up with the industry news of the field or fields that
you either currently work in or want to work in, so that you are
aware of opportunities.** Be in the know right from the beginning

of your career. Subscribe to e-newsletters. Follow your industry leaders on Twitter. Be active in groups on LinkedIn. Go to industry conferences. Read publications for your industry. There are "see and be
seen" opportunities that are really important. For example, go to the
number one, most popular, can't-miss event in your industry—like the
Consumer Electronics Show, if you work in that field.

For more tweaks and resources, go to www.tweakittogether.com/younger
workers.

For older workers

WHY IS IT IMPORTANT FOR OLDER WORKERS TO TWEAK THEIR CAREERS?

Eric Erikson, whose theory of psychosocial development is considered by many to be the gold standard, calls the stage between
forty and sixty-five years old the seventh stage. It's the period
where there's a choice between growing more or stagnating, for
stock taking and refocusing. Most people feel a pull to start creating or caring for things that outlast them, benefit future generations, make the world better, and create a legacy. And if you don't,
you will feel unproductive and less involved. You'll start to lose
your sense of meaning. When I work with older workers, they are
often going through the motions. They are not feeling passionate
about their work anymore. They are thinking about the future and
wanting to reconnect with their sense of inspiration.

—Phyllis Mufson

Tweak: Get back your vitality and what inspires you. Think about
when you were twenty years old. Who was an older person you really
admired? Think about the qualities this person had. Now, here's the
challenge: how do you grow that in you? Start peeling away the layers.

Tweak: Prove wrong any bias about older workers you may experience. For example, people tend to think that people who are older are less technically adept. If you've been in a job a long time, you may be working with older software. You really need to get up to speed. Find out about newer software. Also, become familiar with social media and fill out a complete LinkedIn profile.

Tweak: Find an opportunity to prove you're comfortable working with younger generations. Show that you're okay not being the authority and are willing to listen to others, especially younger people. One way to demonstrate this flexibility is to volunteer for a project where you'll have an opportunity to work with and take direction from people who are younger than you.

For more tweaks and resources, go to www.tweakittogether.com/older workers.

Plan a career break

WHY IS IT IMPORTANT TO PLAN A CAREER BREAK?

There are people who contemplate a career break and have enough foresight to think, *In my future I might take a career break. What are the things that I need to do so I'm in a good position when I'm at the beginning of that career break to maximize my success and return to exactly where I want to be?* If you think about that time out of the workforce in advance, you're more likely to end up at the other end of your career break in a situation where you are happy.

—Carol Fishman Cohen

Tweak: Before you take any career break, first ask if you can work differently. You might be able to put off or not need to take a complete break at all. Present a plan to your manager to work flexibly.

(You will find a step-by-step guide to create a flexible work plan in Cali Yost's first book, *Work+Life: Finding the Fit That's Right for You*.) Don't assume the answer will be no. But if you decide to continue planning for a break...

Tweak: Nurture your current relationships. Not just peer relationships or people whom you report to who are senior to you; be aware of and nurture relationships with people who are junior to you, who report to you, or whom you mentor. Ultimately, those junior people will be moving up while you're on the career break and can be a great resource when you return.

Tweak: Identify opportunities to develop transferable skills. It could be skills in sales, negotiation, or another language. Regardless, learn skills while you're still working that you can take from industry to industry, being mindful that certain skills are more easily transferable than others.

Tweak: Think about how you are going to stay engaged while on break. Cover for others who go on maternity leave, or work on seasonal or special projects. Go to conferences or reunions. People shy away from these opportunities while on break, but they are easy ways to stay in touch.

For more tweaks and resources, go to www.tweakittogether.com/plan careerbreak.

Find an encore (preretirement) career

WHY IS IT IMPORTANT TO TWEAK YOUR SEARCH FOR AN ENCORE (PRERETIREMENT) CAREER?

With increased longevity and the life span of a career, it's easier to plan your legacy. You have time to not just *leave* a legacy but to *live* a legacy. Many people aren't able to retire completely, but they either don't want to or can't work the way they did. You have time to start thinking about how you can set yourself up with a career that pays you and lets you commit to a cause you are passionate about.

—Marci Alboher

Tweak: Read about and research encore careers. Learn more about this new life stage. Read my new book, *The Encore Career Handbook*, and the book by our founder, Marc Freedman, *The Big Shift: Navigating the New Stage beyond Midlife*. Spend time on the www.encore.org website. Check out the stories of the Purpose Prize winners, "like" the Facebook page, and join the LinkedIn group.

Tweak: Self-assess and reconnect to an old passion or discover a new one. Is there a problem or an issue in the world that you want to address? Great sites for inspiration include www.change.org and www .idealist.org. Also, go to the Purpose Prize page at www.encore.org/ prize/ and pick three videos of the winners to watch. Jot down your reactions and see if a story resonates.

Tweak: Answer the question "What are you looking for in the next stage of your life and career?" Are there changes you want to make outside of work? Where you live, the type of people you socialize with, the amount of leisure time you have? What do you need to do to accomplish these goals?

Tweak: Review your finances. An encore career could involve a reduction in income. With that in mind, how far away are you from being able to start an encore career financially? What trade-offs are you able and willing to make in order to work at what matters to you?

For more tweaks and resources, go to www.tweakittogether.com/encore career.

Start your own business

WHY IS IT IMPORTANT TO TWEAK YOUR PLANS TO START YOUR OWN BUSINESS?

People underestimate how much you can do before you've actually "opened your doors." There is valuable information that can get you started on the right foot. Research and plan. The only way to know if entrepreneurship is right for you is to try it in a small, low-risk way. What better way to do that then when you already have your job? I work with a lot of people who have gotten so fed up with their jobs that they act impulsively and quit. But if you do your research and planning, everything you learn is going to further strengthen your business when you get started.

—Adelaide Lancaster

Tweak: Set aside a dedicated time to plan. Carve out a spot during the week that's your time to do this. Establish a routine and you'll have something to look forward to.

Tweak: Meet other entrepreneurs. A lot of people build up in their minds what being an entrepreneur looks like, but you need to understand the reality. Find three to five people from your extended network, take them out to coffee, and discover what the real experience is like.

Tweak: Become a student of three dream businesses you admire. Identify three businesses, not in your industry, that you admire and that are relatively new. These are businesses that run just like you want to run your business two years from now. Follow them on Facebook and Twitter. Read their websites. Get their newsletters. Pay attention to them in the news. What do they do? How do they communicate with their customers? What kinds of promotions are they running?

Tweak: Every week, make a list of what you know and what you don't know. Use that to focus your research efforts. This list will change over time. You might start with "I know I want to work for myself and I know I want to do something with food." But "What I don't know is whether I want to make the food or whether I'd like to sell the food." So this week you are going to research food preparation. Over time, more and more things will move into the "What I know" column as your idea becomes more solid.

For more tweaks and resources, go to www.tweakittogether.com/starta business.

Chapter 13

Money Tweaks

If you seek an everyday foundation of well-being and order in your work and life, then making your personal finances a priority is critical. But as with many other aspects of our lives, it's so easy to get overwhelmed and let it go until a crisis forces us to refocus. Only to take our eye off the personal finance ball again until panic hits once more. It's time to break the cycle. This is particularly true for retirement and college planning.

Retirement—what it looks like, when you take it, and how it's funded—is one of the expectations most radically transformed by the historic work+life changes we've experienced over the last twenty years. It requires time, attention, and resources many years before we will actually retire, if we ever do.

For many parents, saving for college can feel like another unattainable, overwhelming responsibility, so it becomes one of those things you just put off until faced with the reality of a child rapidly approaching college age. If you start early, the burden is much lighter.

The experts in this chapter will help you make managing your personal finances part of your weekly *Tweak It* practice and stop bouncing from crisis to crisis:

- **Everyday Finances:** Manisha Thakor (www.manishathakor.com), author of *Get Financially Naked* and creator of the MoneyZen™ approach to personal finance
- **Retirement Savings:** Mark Miller (www.retirementrevised.com), author of *The Hard Times Guide to Retirement Security*, retirement columnist
- **College Savings:** Joseph Hurley, author of *The Best Way to Save for College—A Complete Guide to 529 Plans* and founder of Saving forCollege.com

Everyday finances

WHY IS IT IMPORTANT TO MANAGE YOUR EVERYDAY PERSONAL FINANCES?

A lot of people don't *equate money problems to other kinds of pain that they feel*. For example, personal finances can be exactly like a cracked tooth. At first you might think it's not a big deal. But then an infection sets in and suddenly you're in excruciating pain and need emergency root-canal surgery. If we're brutally honest, the reason to manage your personal finances is to spare yourself this kind of excruciating pain down the road. A visit to the dentist when the tooth first has a little cavity or crack is so much less painful than what happens when it is ignored.

—Manisha Thakor

Tweak: Figure out what you earn and what goes out the door each month. Don't create a wildly detailed budget, just find two simple numbers—what you earn and what must go out the door each month. You'll have a frame of reference against which to measure your progress.

Tweak: Start to exercise your saving muscle. Start saving. Decide it is a habit you want to develop, even if it's $10 a month. The key is to automate it so that once you've made the decision to save, it just happens.

Tweak: Start investing. Pick a fund with a name like "Target Date 2050" that corresponds to the year in which you'll be hitting retirement age. You invest in that fund, and over time the fund manager gradually shifts allocations among stocks, bonds, and cash.

Tweak: Protect yourself with insurance. Your number one priority is to protect your family. Get term insurance, which is relatively inexpensive. Next protect your home and car. Finally, protect your legacy. Draft a will. You can go to a site like NOLO.com or legalzoom.com for a basic will that will work for most people's situations.

For more tweaks and resources, go to www.tweakittogether.com/every dayfinance.

Retirement savings

WHY IS IT IMPORTANT TO MANAGE YOUR RETIREMENT SAVINGS?

It's important because we're doing such a lousy job of planning for retirement now. Most of the statistics suggest that the average amount that people have saved in either a workplace retirement plan or in a stand-alone IRA averages about $60,000. We have a certain amount of social safety in programs like Social Security and Medicare. Unfortunately, it's probably a pretty good bet that the value of those programs will erode over time. Therefore, it's important to have other resources available, either in the form of savings or other types of insurance. The earlier you start planning the better. All of the data suggests that the younger you start the easier it is.

—Mark Miller

Tweak: Understand your Social Security benefits. Social Security is the single most important lifelong retirement benefit that most Americans will receive. It used to be that Social Security mailed out an annual statement, but that was eliminated as part of budget cutting. There's a great tool on the Social Security website called the Retirement Estimator that you can use to run what-if calculations varying the age you expect to retire.

Tweak: Look at and audit your workplace retirement account, most typically a 401(k). A lot of people are in the habit of setting it and forgetting it. This is not a great idea. You need to check on your savings periodically. It's good to rebalance your assets quarterly if you can, but at least annually. This means if you've determined that you're going to be 70 percent in stocks and 30 percent in bonds or fixed income, that that's going to get unbalanced over time as markets move. Also, take a look at your contribution level. We've seen a growth in the use of automatic enrollment in 401(k) plans, where when you start a job you're defaulted into the plan. But with auto enrollment, oftentimes the default contribution levels are pretty low, averaging around 3 percent of pay. That's too low. See what you can do to max that out and be on a path to increase it annually.

For more tweaks and resources, go to www.tweakittogether.com/retirementsavings.

College savings

WHY IS IT IMPORTANT TO MANAGE YOUR COLLEGE SAVINGS?

Too many parents wait until their child is in high school before they think about how to finance their college education. This produces a lot of anxiety and stress for both the parent and the child. If you take the time now to set up a college savings account and make regular contributions to it, this removes much of the anxiety. For a high school senior, the college decision is difficult enough. Having adequate savings will help get your child to the college that is right for him or her, and not necessarily the college that can come up with the best financial aid package.

—Joseph Hurley

(Note: The 529 Plans that Hurley specializes in are one of the simplest, most straightforward vehicles for saving for college; however, please check with your financial advisor if you want to explore other options that might be right for you and your family.)

Tweak: Go to your state's website for its 529 college savings plan and read about how they work and the benefits they provide. Find a directory of plans at www.savingforcollege.com.

Tweak: Understand that you can shop around for 529 plans offered by other states, but this will take more effort on your part.

Tweak: Open an account with a 529 plan and sign up for automatic monthly contributions, even if only $25 per month. Select the plan's age-based investment option unless you have a specific reason to select a different option.

Tweak: Let your child know about the 529 plan. He or she will remember you are saving with the expectation they will go to some form of higher education, and perhaps even be motivated by it.

For more tweaks and resources, go to www.tweakittogether.com/collegesavings.

Chapter 14

Connect Tweaks

Many of us struggle to truly connect with the people we care about and love. That assumes you've found the time to date or meet people. You may live in the same house as your partner, or see your family members on a regular basis, but do you really know them? It's easy to operate on automatic pilot. The good news is that the experts in this chapter will explain how small, manageable activities and priorities can connect you with loved ones, friends, dates, and your community as part of your weekly *Tweak It* routine:

- **Loved Ones:** Esther Perel (www.estherperel.com), relationship expert and international best-selling, award-winning author of *Mating in Captivity: Unlocking Erotic Intelligence*
- **Friends:** Irene Levine, PhD (www.thefriendshipblog.com), the "Friendship Doctor" and award-winning author of *Best Friends Forever: Surviving a Breakup with Your Best Friend*

- **Date:** Thomas Edwards, founder of the dating site The Professional Wingman (www.theprofessionalwingman.com) and *Maxim* blogger
- **Community:** Courtney Martin (www.courtneyemartin.com), journalist and author of *Do It Anyway: The New Generation of Activists*

Loved ones

WHY IS IT IMPORTANT TO CONNECT WITH YOUR LOVED ONES?

Fundamentally, we derive tremendous meaning from our relationships, with the people that matter to us and for whom we matter, whether it's your friends or your family. People are complacent about their intimate relationships, perhaps more than about any other aspect of their lives. They think relationships will just somehow exist on their own in a for-granted state, and they don't. You know, 50 percent of first marriages end in divorce and 65 percent of second marriages. People really need to understand the small, special things they can do to improve their relationships.

—Esther Perel

Tweak: Create a private e-mail address, a kind of a "lovers' box." This is an e-mail address that nobody else knows about, not even the kids. You can also have a friend box. Some people have used it to send each other songs and music and little flirtatious notes and quotes. It's the one place where you cannot talk about your job or family life or tasks or chores.

Tweak: One day a week, turn off your technology and just be present with your partner or your friends. You need to let people see their value. Relationships are not like cactuses; they don't survive in a drought. You can be at home together with your partner or you can even go for dinner on your weekly date, but if you're going to spend it on your device, what's the point?

Tweak: Embrace the element of surprise. Plan something unexpected. Plan a small trip. It can be a trip to the city. It doesn't have to be something big. Just tell him, "Meet me at eight o'clock. I took care of everything. I got appointments for a massage, tickets to the show, reservations for dinner…" The point is that not everything needs to be negotiated.

For more tweaks and resources, go to www.tweakittogether.com/lovedones.

Friends

WHY IS IT IMPORTANT TO CONNECT WITH YOUR FRIENDS?

Having the support of close friendships helps decrease the risk of depression, and reduce stress. Researchers have found it lowers blood pressure, decreases your cholesterol, and lowers your heart rate. In fact, a study of Australians found that people who had a strong network of friends lived 22 percent longer. So longevity is another reason to have friends. Emotionally, having friends makes us feel connected, makes us feel understood. It's just wonderful to be able to laugh with someone, to share, and to have someone to problem-solve with. Many people say, "My spouse is my best friend." Yet, your spouse may not have all of the same interests as you do. Friends complement your spousal relationship.

—Irene Levine, PhD

Tweak: Schedule time for friendship the way you would schedule a doctor's appointment. If you find that your friendships are sliding, work it into your schedule. Write it in ink. The idea of "let's get together" is vague and meaningless because nothing ever happens unless you make it concrete.

Tweak: Do double duty. Do an activity with a friend. If you feel crunched for time, accomplish something with a friend at the same time. Do your supermarket shopping or go to the gym with a friend. Having relationships doesn't always have to create an additional pressure. One woman told me that she used her treadmill time to talk on the phone with her long-distance friend.

Tweak: Challenge your resistance to making friends in your workplace. Some people think that work and friendship don't mix. They are very strict about separating the two. If you're spending a large portion of your day working, that attitude really eliminates a tremendous source of potential friends. While there are some risks and you need to proceed somewhat cautiously, it's really important to cultivate workplace friendships. There are studies that show that people who have friends in the workplace are more productive and happy employees.

For more tweaks and resources, go to www.tweakittogether.com/friends.

Date

WHY IS IT IMPORTANT TO FIND TIME TO DATE?

It's pretty straightforward: If you don't find time to date, then you're not going to date. If you're looking to settle down in hopes of creating a family, that's something that's going to take time. The time you put in is going to contribute directly to the quality of your dating life. Although dating requires time, it doesn't mean that you can't be efficient.

—Thomas Edwards

Tweak: Identify activities or groups that you can contribute to or just want to get involved in. Look at the issues or groups that you're passionate about. See if there are groups in your area or events that are going on where you can meet like-minded people. Once you pick a group or an activity, be as active in them as possible. These events offer a natural icebreaker, whether it's a social group at a sports club or it's a foodie event.

Tweak: Become friends with someone of the opposite gender.
People love to matchmake, and nowadays people prefer to meet their
future match through mutual friends. The matchmaking can work
both ways, so it should be a mutually beneficial relationship.

**Tweak: Look at where you spend a lot of time and for opportuni-
ties to meet people.** As part of your day-to-day lifestyle, become more
aware of what's going on around you and open yourself up to opportunities that allow you to meet new people. Maybe you spend a lot of time
at a gym or you love yoga. Both could be great places to meet someone.
Pay attention during those experiences and make yourself more open.
It may require you to put down your book and unplug the iPod. But, on
the flip side, those two things could make you more approachable if you
want to meet someone who reads and listens to music.

For more tweaks and resources, go to www.tweakittogether.com/date.

Community

WHY IS IT IMPORTANT TO CONNECT WITH YOUR COMMUNITY?

All of the latest science on happiness shows that it's community ties
and meaningful relationships that make people feel the most joy and
the most fulfilled. Some of us get that joy and fulfillment through
our work lives. But realistically many of us don't, which is why it's so
critical that we use that time outside of work in a way that makes us
feel connected, useful, and really rooted in our own communities.

—Courtney Martin

**Tweak: Reflect and see where your "deep gladness meets deep
need."** "Find where your deep gladness meets the world's deep need,"
wrote theologian Frederick Buechner. Sometimes we think that community work's not going to be enjoyable. Instead, we could think about

what our gift is and how can we give that gift. It's important to reflect about what's going to be fun for us.

Tweak: Create a ritual in your community. We've lost ongoing rituals in our communities, whether it's a book club, a giving circle that meets regularly, or a block party to get the kids in the neighborhood together one day every summer. Any kind of ritual that you can create and people know they can count on to lift their spirits can be really powerful.

Tweak: Find online opportunities to connect with your community. There's a whole movement of people trying to figure out how to use the Internet to get neighbors talking to one another again. It includes everything from Meetup, which is the most widely known, with nine million local groups meeting through it. There's also Front Porch Forum, a local online site for people having community conversations.

For more tweaks and resources, go to www.tweakittogether.com/community.

Chapter 15

Connect with Kids Tweaks

The reality is that most parents work. My husband and I both work full-time and have two children. So we understand firsthand how when you add school, sports, and technology to the mix you can easily end up going through the motions and not stopping to truly know your child. That goes for mothers, fathers, or any adult who, by birth or choice, have children that they love and care for.

The experts in this chapter will show you easy, small steps you can take to connect with the children in your life of all ages and life stages—under thirteen years old, teen, high school, and preparing for college—as part of your weekly *Tweak It* routine:

- **Kids under thirteen years:** Amy McCready (www.positiveparent ingsolutions.com), parenting expert and author of *If I Have to Tell You One More Time ... The Revolutionary Program That Gets Your Kids to Listen without Nagging, Reminding, or Yelling*

- **Teens:** Annie Fox (www.anniefox.com), educator and award-winning author of the *Middle School Confidential*™ series
- **Just for Dads:** Matt Schneider, cofounder of the NYC Dads Group, a resource/community for dads; Bruce Sallan, "A Dad's Point-of-View" columnist, radio show and Twitter #DadChat host
- **Nieces/Nephews:** Melanie Notkin (www.SavvyAuntie.com), author of *Savvy Auntie: The Ultimate Guide for Cool Aunts, Great-Aunts, Godmothers, and All Women Who Love Kids* (Note: This advice applies to uncles, or FUNcles, too.)
- **Technology:** Shawn Edgington (www.shawnedgington.com), cyberbullying prevention expert and author of *The Parent's Guide to Texting, Facebook, and Social Media*
- **School:** Angela Maiers (www.angelamaiers.com), educator and author of *Classroom Habitudes*
- **College Planning:** John Carpenter (www.askjohnaboutcollege .com), author of *Going Geek: What Every Smart Kid (and Every Smart Parent) Should Know about College Admissions*
- **SAT Prep:** Debbie Stier, founder of the Perfect Score Project (www .perfectscoreproject.com)

Kids under thirteen years old

WHY IS IT IMPORTANT TO CONNECT WITH THE CHILDREN IN YOUR LIFE WHO ARE UNDER THIRTEEN YEARS OLD?

Kids, both the little and the big, have a hard-wired need for emotional connection and positive attention. If we don't take time to fill their emotional needs with positive focus and meaningful connections, they find ways to get us to notice. Younger children usually do this with negative attention-seeking behaviors like whining, clinging, or dragging out the bedtime routine. Older kids tend to become less cooperative. They do the opposite of what we want them to. They may backtalk or have an attitude. Parents can avoid so many negative behaviors if they take time to emotionally connect, be there, and be totally present on a daily basis.

—Amy McCready

Tweak: Find "mind, body, and soul" time with your child. Spend at least ten minutes per day with each child in one-on-one time. During the ten minutes be fully present in mind, body, and soul. You're not thinking about your to-do list, and the BlackBerry goes in the briefcase. This gives children a big dose of positive attention, which we know that they have to have. And it gives them that emotional connection, because you're saying, "I want to do whatever you want to do. I want to get into your world and do what is important to you."

Tweak: Practice using your calm voice. One of the biggest frustrations parents have, especially busy working parents, is that they're constantly in a rush. We have to get things done, "chop, chop, chop," and we end up raising our voices and yelling. When you talk with your kids, slow your voice down and lower the volume a little bit.

Tweak: Say yes more often. Find opportunities to say yes. For example, instead of saying, "No, we can't go to the park today. We have too much to do," you can say, "The park sounds awesome, but today is not such a good day. Do you think we should go after school on Friday or over the weekend?" You're presenting the answer in a way that's a yes.

For more tweaks and resources, go to www.tweakittogether.com/kids under13.

Teens

WHY IS IT IMPORTANT TO CONNECT WITH THE TEENS IN YOUR LIFE?

Teens are constantly connected to their peers and to their contemporaries via text and Facebook, but in many ways they are very disconnected. They need some balance in those connections that includes caring, trusted adults. They need us. Their other connections are not like the one they have with their parents. We always have our teens' best interest in mind, which can't always be said for the people that they call their "friends."

—Annie Fox

Tweak: Have dinner with your family at least three times a week. It doesn't matter what you're eating. We are not talking about a Martha Stewart or Top Chef dinner. What matters is that you sit down together, turn off the phones, and look each other in the eyes and talk. For parents that includes listening. The research shows that kids who have dinner with their parents at least three times a week are less likely to engage in high-risk behavior. They get better grades. They are just all around more grounded kids.

Tweak: Talk less and listen more. Teens are changing before our eyes. If you are not listening, then you're missing all of the insights that will help you understand how your young person is progressing toward adulthood. Pay attention. Ask a question and then close your mouth. Use an open-ended question. An observation will give you an opportunity to listen: "You seem a little down. What's going on?"

Tweak: Catch your teen in the act of doing something right. When you catch your teen in the act of doing something right, it adds something positive to the relationship. Your teen is never too old, too jaded, or too cool to hear someone say, "I really appreciate what you just did." For example, if you see him helping a little brother or sister with homework and you didn't ask him to do it, don't make a big deal about it, just say, "That was really nice."

For more tweaks and resources, go to www.tweakittogether.com/teens.

Just for Dads

WHY IS IT IMPORTANT FOR DADS TO CONNECT WITH THE CHILDREN IN THEIR LIVES?

Pioneering fathers need to break down the walls that say men can't be serious about their careers and still be serious about their families. I've seen a lot of examples of men who sneak out of the office. They say that they have a doctor's appointment rather than that they're going to pick up their kids at school. What these dads aren't saying is, "I'm going to be a leader at our firm and tell everyone that leaving at 4:30 p.m. is fine," because they can prioritize both work and family equally.

—Matt Schneider

Tweak: Detach from your technology. Technology is forcing us to be available 24/7, and we're the only ones that can set boundaries. If you are with your child, be with your child without the distraction of your BlackBerry, iPhone, or laptop.

Tweak: Find time to play. Enjoy the time you have with your kids. Roughhousing is a terrific way to laugh and connect.

I don't care if you're a dad or a mom, in the end the thing that will give you enduring happiness and make you feel your life was worthwhile are the relationships you build with your own family primarily, and secondarily the good you do in the world.

—Bruce Sallan

Tweak: Schedule a time to do something special. The more time you spend with your kids, the more they'll open up to you. Depending on what your schedule allows, do something special with one or more of the kids and then add to it as you find you love it.

Tweak: Create a sharing ritual. During our Friday night dinners we go around the table and everybody shares the best and the worst things that happened to them in the previous week.

For more tweaks and resources, go to www.tweakittogether.com/justfor dads.

Nieces/Nephews

WHY IS IT IMPORTANT FOR AUNTS, UNCLES, AND GODPARENTS TO CONNECT WITH THE CHILDREN IN THEIR LIVES?

Family is not what it was many years ago. In fact, parents need secondary caretakers, or "Savvy Aunties," and FUNcles now more than ever. We need to remix the way things were back when families all took care of each other and where every woman was a maternal figure in the village. Yes, babies come from the womb, but maternity comes from the soul. There are many ways to mother. Today, every child needs many mothers in their lives. Every little hand we hold, every boo-boo we kiss, and every hug we give is a gift. And we should all feel appreciated and valued for what we do.

—Melanie Notkin

Tweak: Schedule uninterrupted "qual-Auntie" or FUNcle time. Unlike parents, time we spend with a niece or nephew is often specifically cut out for the aunt/uncle and that child or children. It's uninterrupted time. So right away the child feels special. In fact, uninterrupted attention from grown-ups is one of the key drivers to helping develop a baby or young child's sense of security. Now, this means putting down that iPhone for a little while, but what you create in return is invaluable. Often a child remembers the time they spent with an aunt or uncle as magical. (For ideas of how to spend your "qual-Auntie" time go to www.SavvyAuntie.com.)

Tweak: Take a niece or nephew to a special place. For example, in New York City we have the Plaza Hotel. Go with your niece and dress up for the occasion. Look for Eloise in the hotel. Teach her a couple of French words. That will feel magical. Treat her to a cup of hot chocolate in one of the snack bars or restaurants in the hotel. One of the Savvy Auntie principles is "parents rule," but assuming the parents are okay letting you give their child a first experience, you could take your nephew to his first baseball game.

For more tweaks and resources, go to www.tweakittogether.com/nieces nephews.

Technology

WHY IS IT IMPORTANT TO CONNECT WITH THE CHILDREN IN YOUR LIFE ABOUT TECHNOLOGY?

> When it comes to teens and social media, talking to friends in social networking communities and playing games can be completely risk-free and good fun. But there's also the danger of online predators, cyberbullies, sexting, online harassment, and locating adult websites that we need to keep a watchful eye on.
>
> —Shawn Edgington

Tweak: Execute a "rules of engagement" cell phone and Internet contract to set their online boundaries. Remind your kids that once they post information online, they can't take it back, and to set their privacy settings to "Private." Discuss the importance of managing their online reputation and brand—it's more important than ever before.

Tweak: Learn how to monitor all of your teen's social networking sites. Log on using their user name and password (which they must give you), and watch what information they're posting and read their comments. If your child is under thirteen, they should *not* have a Facebook account.

Tweak: Set a Google alert for each of your children's names. Go to www.google.com/alerts to get e-mail updates when your child's name is mentioned online.

Tweak: Ask your child if they've felt threatened or uncomfortable as a result of something happening online or by text. Start the dialogue by encouraging your teens to confide in you. Encourage your teen to trust their gut if they have suspicions regarding unsolicited requests from strangers. Make sure they block and report any offender.

Tweak: Talk to your teens about inappropriate sex talk online. Tell them that it won't be tolerated by you. Emphasize that you are doing this for his or her own good, as this kind of thing can escalate into a dangerous real-world situation.

For more tweaks and resources, go to www.tweakittogether.com/kids andtech.

School

WHY IS IT IMPORTANT TO CONNECT WITH YOUR CHILDREN'S SCHOOL AND EDUCATION?

It's about attitude and engagement. Be engaged in the mission to make education a priority in your child's life. It means you are involved physically, mentally, and emotionally. Parents must let their kids know no matter what they're going through at school, no matter what the challenge is, that they matter and their education matters. We have to recognize that our attitude about education, and its role in our own lives, is how we communicate our love and passion for learning to our children.

—Angela Maiers

Tweak: Go to your school's website. Learn about the school and your child's teacher(s). I am surprised how few parents look at the school's website. Spend fifteen minutes reading about your school's philosophy, goals, and mission. Learn about your child's teacher or teachers. Of course, you want to meet your child's teacher face-to-face, but it's not always possible. But many teachers have their own individual web pages, and you can learn a lot there. If you have young children, you can build a relationship with one teacher when you drop them off or pick them up. It can get overwhelming, however, if your child sees up to seven teachers throughout the day. It isn't necessary to get to know all of them. Pick an advisor or a homeroom teacher. Focus on getting to know the teacher in the class your child might struggle with the most.

Tweak: Find out how your school is going to communicate with you. Sit down and take thirty minutes to map out the different information streams and the kinds of questions that will probably come up in the year. This can be a challenge if there are multiple streams of communication, but many of your questions can get answered if you look in the right place. The information you'll get on your school's Facebook page is going to be different from the kind of information you'll find on its website. If you have questions about assignments, you're not going to go to the Facebook page. If you have questions about school delays, you're not going to go to the website. You're going to where the information is immediate.

For more tweaks and resources, go to www.tweakittogether.com/school.

College Planning

WHY IS IT IMPORTANT TO CONNECT WITH YOUR CHILD'S COLLEGE SEARCH PROCESS?

It's important for the parent and student to work together on the college process—not just the parent. It has to be a project involving mutual coordination and planning. Parents need to feel linked in to the process, and to understand what the hoops are that their kids are expected to jump through. They need to understand the emotional demands being put on kids so they can also know how to support them.

—John Carpenter

Tweak: Establish a regular weekly time to sit down and talk about college admissions, and ...

Tweak: Commit to *not* talking about college the rest of the week. About halfway through junior year of high school, establish a regular time to talk about college once a week, and then agree to not talk about it at other times.

Tweak: Read, read, read about the college admissions. Stick with published books and university websites. Avoid any website that is social media based, because you can get *lost* wading through dozens of opinions that are not based on anything other than rumors, gossip, and hearsay. For better time management, choose two or three reputable resources, and skip the rest.

Tweak: Schedule an appointment with your child's high school guidance counselor early on. See who your partner will be in this is process. Also, be clear with your questions and in your commitment to support the counselor. Let him or her know as much about your child as possible, including your child's strengths.

Tweak: Agree early on with your child on a range of outcomes that are acceptable to both of you. But be flexible, as circumstances that might affect those outcomes change throughout the process.

For more tweaks and resources, go to www.tweakittogether.com/college.

SAT/Testing Prep

WHY IS IT IMPORTANT TO CONNECT WITH THE CHILD'S SAT PROCESS?

The summer before junior year is when you need to start really preparing. Your child needs to know the information in the SAT in a deep way so that he or she can recall it and use it during the test. That's why the preparation needs to be long-term and practiced. It's not a fast process, and unfortunately schools are not, in general, teaching as deeply as they should for kids to do well.

—Debbie Stier

Tweak: Sign up to receive the College Board Question of the Day. When your child reaches ninth grade, you and your child should go to the College Board site (sat.collegeboard.org) and sign up to receive the Question of the Day. The questions you receive are easy to midrange, but at least it's a shared conversation you can have together every day: "Did you get that vocab right?" It's like Trivial Pursuit.

Tweak: Get the College Board Blue Book, the *Official SAT Study Guide.* When your child reaches ninth or tenth grade, order this book of ten official tests put out by the College Board. It's as close as you're going to get to the actual test. Familiarize yourself with the tests and start pointing out the vocabulary words. It's a natural way to start preparing early without your child saying, "Mom, it's too early for SAT test prep."

Tweak: Map out the SAT process on a calendar starting the summer after sophomore year through the summer before senior year. Once your child chooses the day they want to take the test:

- Input your zip code and choose the school where your child wants to take the test. You want to do this early because a lot of the schools fill up.

- Test conditions matter greatly. Start asking around about the different schools. "What size desks to they have? Do they have the little deskette or do they have the normal-size desk?"
- Help your child know their test rights. For example, you are entitled to a quiet environment. My son knows to say something if there's noise.

For more tweaks and resources, go to www.tweakittogether.com/sat.

Chapter 16

Caregiving Tweaks

If I ruled the world, all working families and adult children of aging parents would have access to affordable, reliable child care and elder care. But I don't rule the world; therefore, it's still up to us to plan for the everyday care of our children and adult relatives.

Unfortunately, my experience over the past two decades has been that we don't take enough time to carefully and thoughtfully plan for all of our caregiving needs. We wait until a crisis occurs and then frantically search for options that may not be good for our loved ones or for us. Don't wait. The experts in this chapter will share simple, get-started steps for taking an organized approach to caregiving as part of your weekly *Tweak It* routine:

- **Elder Care—General:** Denise M. Brown, author of *The Working Family Caregiver* and founder of Caregiving.com

- **Elder Care—with Siblings:** Francine Russo (www.yourparents too.com), author of *They're Your Parents Too!: How Siblings Can Survive Their Parents' Aging without Driving Each Other Crazy*
- **Child Care:** Sheila Lirio Marcelo, CEO of Care.com
- **Summer Care:** Jill Tipograph (www.everythingsummer.com), author of *Your Everything Summer™ Guide & Planner*

Elder Care—General

WHY IS IT IMPORTANT TO THINK ABOUT ELDER CARE EVEN BEFORE IT'S AN ISSUE?

When the need for elder care arrives, you can be faced with chaos. The amount of time it takes to organize help and solutions can overwhelm. And the emotional toll of elder care—your emotions, your aging relative's emotions—can be exhausting and, sometimes, paralyzing. If you're not prepared for what could happen with aging relatives, you'll make tough decisions during a time of crisis. And it's not just one crisis you potentially have to manage, but a series of crises over several years. We often assume that the government is going to pay for the care. Elder care is not something that's covered by Medicare. You and or your family member have to pay for it. I've worked in this field since 1990, and people were shocked then and they're still shocked today that there's no government support. So you have to have a plan.

—Denise M. Brown

Tweak: Ask aging relatives about their wishes. Understanding what they want will help guide you as you make decisions on their behalf. Be sure to have a durable Power of Attorney for health care and finance for them. A great resource to help you is called *Five Wishes* (www.aging withdignity.org), a worksheet to document end-of-life care issues.

Tweak: Understand your budget for care. Start with the premise that nothing is covered, because really and truly nothing is unless you qualify for Medicaid. Medicare benefits for long-term care are very narrow and short-term. Most likely either you or your aging relative will have to pay. Recognize that elder care can last much longer than you think it will. Build that possibility into your budget.

Tweak: Get support in person and virtually. Find others' caregivers to talk with about your worries and your frustrations. Talking will make the tough times more manageable. The Eldercare Locator website (www.eldercare.gov) can tell you about support groups that are in your community.

For more tweaks and resources, go to www.tweakittogether.com/eldercare.

Elder Care—Coordinating with Siblings

WHY IS IT IMPORTANT TO CONNECT AND COORDINATE WITH YOUR SIBLINGS ABOUT ELDER CARE?

Our parents' aging brings up deep and old feelings from childhood. And there is a temptation for high-energy, hard workers to be the one to take everything on and think, *I can do this, I'll take care of Mom. I'll take care of Dad.* But, in fact, it becomes an overwhelming task. Also there's a risk that if you do it all that will foster resentment and bad feelings among your siblings. They will feel left out, rightfully. It's important, wherever possible, for the family to get on the same page and share some responsibilities, or at least share their feelings about the experience.

—Francine Russo

Tweak: Call a family meeting with your siblings and your parents. Get in the same room and hear what your parents want in terms of their health-care wishes. If only one person hears it, then there is a possibility down the road of distrust, disbelief, and disagreement at very critical junctures.

Tweak: Hire a geriatric care manager or get an advisor from a non-profit, such as a social worker. If the family can afford it, a geriatric-care manager can make this process so much easier. Especially when siblings are in different parts of the country, they will need someone to coordinate care. There's a national association of licensed professional geriatric-care managers.

Tweak: Discuss potential or actual divisions of responsibilities. There is an overwhelming tendency for one person to do everything. With a little imagination and cooperation, families can take the burden off the caregiver if the caregiver is willing for it to happen. For example, somebody could do all the financial and insurance work even from a distance. If Mom is housebound and needs groceries delivered, somebody else could organize that. Somebody could be in charge of researching medical treatments and approaches and call a meeting with the family to discuss the medical options based on the research.

For more tweaks and resources, go to www.tweakittogether.com/elder care.

Child Care

WHY IS IT IMPORTANT TO PLAN FOR YOUR REGULAR AND BACKUP CHILD-CARE NEEDS?

A comprehensive care plan lets you be more focused at work and more present at home. Building a solid care structure that gives you some flexibility requires time and effort to establish—you can't take shortcuts with this. And last-minute planning causes stress in relationships and at work, and affects our well-being. Daily planning isn't just to ensure that meals and activities for your child get done; coordinating with your care provider develops trust between how the two of you work together in partnership.

—Sheila Lirio Marcelo

Tweak: Create a job posting that clearly states your needs, from any special issues and desired skills to how much you'd like to pay. Be very clear, because spelling everything out saves you time. Samples are available at Care.com.

Tweak: Run stringent background checks when you find some care providers who seem interesting. Check references. Whether you use a website like Care.com, post an ad in the library, or a friend refers someone, don't take shortcuts.

Tweak: Prepare an interview checklist of things that are important to you, from food and activities to discipline. Be prepared and go through everything.

Tweak: Plan to spend a few hours with each care provider—both you and your child. Pay particular attention to how they engage with your children and how they respond to your questions.

Tweak: Create a list of favorites for backup care. On Care.com there is an actual "Favorites" application where you screen and begin to interview backup babysitters for some date nights and other events to give them a test run, so when you need someone you aren't just inviting a stranger into your home. Rotate among a few sitters. Don't always use the same sitter, so you have two or three people whom you can comfortably call on.

For more tweaks and resources, go to www.tweakittogether.com/child care.

Summer Child Care

WHY IS IT IMPORTANT TO PLAN FOR YOUR SUMMER CHILD-CARE NEEDS?

In today's world, it's important to have structure in a child's summer, just as there's structure during the year. If you're a busy working parent, you have to be in control of creating that schedule and it can be a lot of work. But the difference between school and summer is that in the summer you get to pick and choose what your child does. During the year, so much of that is decided for you. The summer takes planning, but the longer you wait the less likely it will be that you will be able to find them a place in the camp or summer program or your choice.

—Jill Tipograph

Tweak: Start planning for next summer with a recap at the end of the most recent summer. How was this summer? Did the schedule and the activities work for my child? Did they work for me? Did they work for us as a family? What would we do differently?

Tweak: At the end of each summer start a summer savings plan. Consider putting aside $10 or $20 a week in a dedicated savings account, depending on what you will need for the program of your choice. Also, for your child's birthdays or holidays, you may want to consider asking grandparents and other relatives to give money toward the summer fund.

Tweak: In the fall, do your research. When you're not under a lot of pressure in the fall, talk to people, consider alternatives, and collect information. Have conversations with the people who run the programs you are interested in to make sure it's a fit. Evaluate your finances.

Tweak: In early winter, commit to the best option. Once you've chosen the dates, reserve a place in the program or camp that seems best to fit your child's needs.

Tweak: Plan your family vacation *after* your children have their summer scheduled. Oftentimes parents unknowingly plan a vacation in the middle of two camp sessions, and it prevents their child from being able to do either.

For more tweaks and resources, go to www.tweakittogether.com/summercare.

Chapter 17

Maintenance Tweaks

If there's one area where we waste the most time and energy and where weekly tweaks could have the most direct and immediate impact, it's in the day-to-day maintenance of ourselves, our homes, and our cars. I'd be wealthy if I had a dollar for every time I heard someone make a comment along the lines of "I was late because:

- I couldn't find my keys;
- I couldn't find anything clean to wear;
- I haven't been feeling well;
- My car wouldn't start; or
- My gutters backed up and ruined my ceiling."

If we got regular physicals, planned how we looked, maintained our cars, and kept our homes organized, cleaned, and maintained, we would save ourselves so much wasted time, money, and stress. This doesn't mean that you have to become Martha Stewart. The simple basics will get you far. The experts in this chapter will share small activities and priorities so that you can make maintenance part of your weekly *Tweak It* routine:

- **Your Health:** David Evans, MD, assistant professor of family medicine, University of Washington Medical Center, former president of the National Physicians Alliance
- **Your Personal Appearance:** Bridgette Raes (www.bridgetteraes .com), author of *Style Rx: Dressing the Body You Have to Create the Body You Want*
- **Your Car:** Larry Webster, editor-in-chief of *Road & Track* (www .RoadandTrack.com)
- **Your House—Get Organized:** Lorie Marrero, author of *The Clutter Diet: The Skinny on Organizing Your Home and Taking Control of Your Life*
- **Your House—Clean It Yourself:** Leslie Reichert (www.green cleaningcoach.com), author of *The Joy of Green Cleaning*
- **Your House—Hire Cleaning Help:** Marie Stegner (www.maid brigade.com), consumer health advocate for Maid Brigade, Inc.
- **Your House—Maintain It:** Harry Sawyers, associate editor of *Popular Mechanics* (www.popularmechanics.com)

Your Health

WHY IS IT IMPORTANT TO MAINTAIN YOUR HEALTH IN PARTNERSHIP WITH A DOCTOR?

You aren't good to anyone else if you aren't taking care of yourself. There are a variety of preventative, age-related medical tests to make sure you are as healthy as you can be. For example, vaccines, mammograms, pap smears, and colonoscopies are required for good health. The mistakes I see most people make are not keeping up with their preventative health-care needs and waiting too long when something doesn't feel right to get it checked. Most people are in tune with their bodies and know when things don't feel right or abnormal. It's better to go to the doctor and be told nothing is wrong than to ignore it until it's out of control.

—David Evans, MD

Tweak: Find a primary care physician who can communicate with you in a way that works for you. This is the person who will be the quarterback for your health-care team. It's trial and error identifying the best person, but it's helpful to ask your friends. You can find all sorts of rating sites online, but your friends and neighbors are the best source.

Tweak: Understand what your insurance covers. With health-care reform, preventative health care like pap smears, mammograms, and colonoscopies are covered by private health insurance and Medicare without a deductible or co-pay. If you don't have insurance, there are local federally qualified community health centers that have sliding-scale fee agreements with labs and imaging facilities.

Tweak: Find a practice that is open early, late, and on weekends so you don't have to miss work. They do exist.

Tweak: Check reliable websites for a list of tests that are appropriate for your age and gender. Sites include:

http://www.uspreventiveservicestaskforce.org/uspstf/uspsabrecs.htm

http://www.canadiantaskforce.ca/recommendations__past_eng.html

http://www.aafp.org/online/etc/medialib/aafp_org/documents/clinical/CPS/rcps08-2005.Par.0001.File.tmp/May2012.pdf

Tweak: Make appointments to get those tests in a timely manner.

For more tweaks and resources, go to www.tweakittogether.com/yourhealth.

Your Personal Appearance

WHY IS IT IMPORTANT TO PAY ATTENTION TO YOUR PERSONAL APPEARANCE?

> Maintaining your personal appearance is important because what you wear is the strongest form of nonverbal communication. Additionally, self-perception is important. How we perceive ourselves sends a clear message to others. If we feel confident about the way we look it will express confidence and others will get that. Self-care is usually the first thing to go out the window when we are busy, and often this includes how we dress. If we don't focus on our appearance, we often wind up having to work twice as hard to send the proper message than if we just took a little extra time each day.
>
> —Bridgette Raes

Tweak: Know your goals for the day. This can change daily or it can be constant. Before an event—work, a date, an interview, or a night out—think about what your goal is. In particular, think about how you want to feel. Try to come up with three words to describe that feeling. If what you put on doesn't make you feel that way, you're not going to express yourself the way you want to.

Tweak: Organize your closet. It's a simple action, but it can yield great results. Life is busy enough. Having to dig in the morning to find what you want to wear is a time suck. Keep order in your closet; for example, by type of clothing—jackets, skirts, pants, blouses—and then hang clothes from light to dark. Commit to a seasonal closet edit. Purge what isn't working for you any longer.

Tweak: Pick a day of the week for dropping off dry cleaning, shoe repairs, mending, and altering. Add this step to the day you do errands.

Tweak: Review your schedule for the week and think about what you will wear. You'll know if you need to drop off a certain pair of pants for cleaning, and so on, and it alleviates the stress of waking up and feeling like you have nothing to wear.

For more tweaks and resources, go to www.tweakittogether.com/your appearance.

Keep Your Car Running

WHY IS IT IMPORTANT TO MAINTAIN YOUR CAR?

The better you maintain your car, the more it will be there for you. Or conversely, the less you maintain the car, the more problems you will have. The key to car maintenance is to be proactive, not reactive. That's a big thing to remember.

—Larry Webster

Tweak: Clean your car inside and outside on a weekly or monthly basis. Two things will happen. One, it will stop the crud from accumulating, which makes it harder to clean later. But two, cleaning it will get you to inspect your car. You may notice that the tires are starting to wear unevenly, and you can catch the alignment problem before it ruins your tires. Also, if you can remove the salt from the paint, it will look nicer and function better longer.

Tweak: Every month, at least, check your tire pressure and fluid levels. Checking your tire pressure is very simple. Do it first thing in the morning when the car hasn't been driven for a while. That's called cold tire pressure. Get a gauge and look at the tire pressures in your owner's manual. Religiously keep those pressures at the proper level. And while you are doing that, pop the hood and check all the fluid levels. Look for oil, transmission level, coolant, and even washer fluid. If you don't know how to do all that, it's almost universally very clearly and simply explained in the owner's manual.

Tweak: Read the owner's manual. It's your bible. The manufacturer wants you to get the most out of the car you just bought. The owner's manual dictates how to do it. Follow the maintenance schedule in the owner's manual. The repair shops will suggest maintenance schedules that are far more rigorous and expensive than you need.

Tweak: Make sure you are using the right type of gas. Don't use cheap discount gas. Today's cars have fuel injectors that are very precise. Help yourself long-term and pick the name-brand fuel.

For more tweaks and resources, go to www.tweakittogether.com/yourcar.

Organize Your Home

WHY IS IT IMPORTANT TO ORGANIZE YOUR HOME?

When you are organized, there are three big things that you save: time, money, and stress. First, let's talk about money. When you're organized you will have fewer late fees. You will find forgotten charges like the gym membership that you're not using. You make smarter purchases because you know what you have and then you use what you have. You'll save time not having to look for things that are lost. You could have spent that time on your business, on your family, or whatever matters to you, all of which reduces stress.

—Lorie Marrero

Tweak: Create a destination station. Your destination station should be where you come in and out of the house. It's where your keys, your wallet, your purse, your kids' backpacks, and your chargers for your cell phone all go—whatever will help you get it in and out the door more quickly when you don't have to look for it anymore. The destination and errand station could be a row of hooks on a wall; a piece of furniture, like a sideboard; or a closet near the door that you can repurpose.

Tweak: Create a morning and an evening routine. People haven't really thought through their morning and evening routines. Here are two routines. Add the particulars for your family. In the morning, "D-E-W," like the morning dew: Dishes—Eating—Wash. Empty your dishwasher and put all the clean dishes away. Decide in the morning what you're going to eat for dinner and do whatever you can to get that started. Then there's wash, which means put your laundry through to the next step in the cycle. If it's in the washer, put it in the dryer.

Tweak: In the evening, there's the "Triple S." *Start* the dishwasher. *Straighten* up. Do a little clutter patrol. *Set* for tomorrow. Think it through: *What do I need for the morning? Do I have to pack lunches, or just make sure I put my laptop back in my briefcase and put it by the door?*

For more tweaks and resources, go to www.tweakittogether.com/yourhome.

Clean House—Yourself

WHY IS IT IMPORTANT TO CLEAN YOUR HOME?

There are three reasons to stay on top of cleaning and laundry. The first one is for your mental well-being. If your environment is a mess, it's going to affect your mental state. A lot of people that I work with are just out of control in every aspect of their lives. When your house is out of control, it affects everything else in your life. The second reason is physical. You don't want to live in chaos. We call it "can't have anybody over" syndrome. You should not have to run to the door when people ring your door-bell because you don't want to let them in. You should feel good about where you're living. It's your environment. It's your home. The third is for health reasons. If your house is not clean, it can affect the health of you and your family. If you do it for no other reason, than do it for better health.

—Leslie Reichert

Tweak: Follow a simple daily routine to keep your bathroom clean: (1) squeegee out your shower when you're done with it, (2) swish the toilet bowl with the brush, (3) clean the mirror with a microfiber cloth, (4) clean the vanity with the same microfiber cloth, and (5) clean the floor.

Tweak: Try one new, simple cleaning routine a week or a month, depending on how big your space is. The biggest problem for people is that they don't pick up during the week, so then it becomes this huge mountain at the end of the week. For example, one simple routine to start is picking up the family room before everybody goes to bed. It takes you three minutes at the most, but you can go to bed saying, "Okay, I've got at least that room under control."

Tweak: Once a week, get everyone to do a ten-minute tidy-up. I set the timer for ten minutes and I get fifty minutes of cleaning from the five people in my house. That's half of what a professional would take to clean my house. One goes in the bathroom. One goes in the family room. You can dust and vacuum a room in ten minutes. If you do ten or fifteen minutes once a week with the family, that's going to make a huge dent in your cleaning routine.

For more tweaks and resources, go to www.tweakittogether.com/cleanhouse.

Clean House—Hire Help

WHY IS IT IMPORTANT TO GET SOMEONE TO HELP YOU CLEAN YOUR HOME?

By hiring a cleaning service, you add much-needed time and energy back to your schedule. Instead of spending the weekends cleaning floors and scrubbing bathrooms, you could exercise, or spend quality time with your children. You may even catch up on sleep or on other much-needed chores like gardening and maintaining the outside of the house.

—Marie Stegner

Tweak: Because trust is a key factor in deciding whom to hire, ask a friend who they use and about their experiences with their cleaner, or ask the company for references. Read about the company or individual online. Use Internet searches, Facebook, LinkedIn, and/or online review services like Kudzu.com.

Tweak: Make sure you choose a provider that doesn't require micromanaging, otherwise it will consume time rather than free up time. Bad cleaning services can create more hassles, but a good service will improve your quality of life. A good cleaning company will do everything possible to make using the service easy and convenient, like sending appointment reminders, asking for feedback on quality and customer service, and resolving any concerns promptly and professionally.

Tweak: Make sure the company or individual has insurance for damage and theft and especially workman's comp. If they don't have insurance, you could be liable if they slip and fall in the shower or on your driveway. That can be costly.

Tweak: Interview prospective providers much like you would a potential employee. Ask what tasks are included in a typical cleaning and whether you have the flexibility to change the cleaning regimen based on varying needs, such as a seasonal deep cleaning.

For more tweaks and resources, go to www.tweakittogether.com/clean house.

Maintain Your Home

WHY IS IT IMPORTANT TO MAINTAIN YOUR HOME EVERY SEASON?

Popular Mechanics offers a series of monthly and seasonal maintenance checklists for homeowners to follow. Pick your season and follow the suggested steps.

—Harry Sawyers

Tweak: Here is a list of checklists and URL links to get you started:

Autumn Home Checklist: Suggested actions include checking if your gas engine leaf blower will start; bringing firewood in from outside and restacking it; calling for a furnace tune-up (http://www.popularmechanics.com/home/improvement/outdoor projects/3943161?click=main_sr).

Holiday Home Checklist: Suggested actions include turning off and draining exterior faucets; and stocking up on rock salt and other ice-melting materials (http://www.popularmechanics.com/home/improvement/outdoor-projects/4203222?click=main_sr).

For more tweaks and resources, go to www.tweakittogether.com/yourhome.

More Tweak It *Inspiration Resources*

Zen Habits: www.zenhabits.com
The Happiness Project: www.thehappiness-project.com
Real Simple (magazine and online): www.realsimple.com

Check out the *Tweak It* community for more resources: www.tweakit together.com.

Conclusion

Are you ready? Yes, here's a new work+life reality for all of us. Over the past two decades, several technological, demographic, and economic trends have converged and transformed the way we work and live radically. But with *Tweak It*, you don't have to feel like someone forgot to inform you of the new rules of success on and off the job. While this new, modern, often hectic reality may feel like chaos, you can and must be your own advocate. Build a foundation of everyday well-being and order one small, deliberate step at a time. Create a work+life fit that lets you:

- get to the gym, *and* prepare for a meeting;
- catch up on e-mails, *and* meet a friend for coffee;
- cover a coworker's shift, *and* shop for food for the week;
- work overtime, *and* take your mother to the doctor;
- catch up on paperwork, *and* read at your child's school; and
- go to a lunchtime networking event, *and* balance your checkbook.

There's no work/life balance, but *Tweak It* harnesses the secrets of the few who seem to get it all done with ease into a simple practice that makes what matters to you happen every day.

The possibilities are endless and ever-changing, because there's no right answer.

The payoffs of committing to the weekly *Tweak It* practice are many. You are more likely to keep your job and love your life in a competitive, rapidly changing global economy. You'll value and leverage the power of small, manageable actions and priorities that aren't scary or overwhelming in uncertain times. And you'll master technology to achieve the goals *you* want to achieve.

Ultimately, what *Tweak It* success looks like will vary for each of us. It may be increased satisfaction and contentment in a particular area of life that is most important to you right now, whether it's wellness, career, personal finance, relationships, or personal maintenance. Or perhaps the structure of completing the *Tweak It* practice consistently each week will simply give you a greater sense of control.

Just begin. Just *Tweak It*! I will be there with you in the *Tweak It* community seeking inspiration and motivation each week (www.tweakit together.com). I'll share my Tweaks of the Week, but I also want to hear from you. What small, creative actions and priorities do you want to accomplish over the next seven days? Are there other helpful experts and tools that have inspired meaningful tweaks that could help all of us? In the process, let's start the *Tweak It* revolution where what matters most is happening in all of our lives. What small action or priority you are going to start with? I can't wait to hear. Tweak It.

Notes

Introduction

1 Cali Williams Yost, "CFOs See Business Impacts of Work-Life Flexibility, But They Can't Execute for Strategic Benefit," *World at Work Journal* (Second Quarter, 2009): 59–67.

2 "When Work Works: Flex at a Glance," http://whenworkworks.org/research/downloads/FlexAtAGlance.pdf.

3 Liz Watson and Jennifer E. Swanberg, PhD, *Flexible Workplace Solutions for Low-Wage Hourly Workers: A Framework for a National Conversation*, Workplace Flexibility 2010 Georgetown Law and iWin (2011).

4 Cali Williams Yost, "The Workplace Challenges Political Candidates Have to Address," *Fast Company*, April 25, 2012. http://www.fastcompany.com/1834970/workplace-challenges-political-candidates-have-address.

5 Sharon Jayson, "Stress Levels Increased Since 1983, New Analysis Shows," *USA Today*, June, 13, 2012. http://www.usatoday.com/news/health/story/2012-06-13/stress-increase-over-time/55587296/1.

6 Cali Williams Yost, "3 Signs Flexible Work Is Strategic—And Not Just Window Dressing," *Fast Company*, June 14, 2012. http://www.fastcompany.com/1840236/3-signs-flexible-work-strategic-and-not-just-window-dressing.

7 Cali Williams Yost, "The 10 Keys to Building the Flexible Workplace of the Future," *The Atlantic*, July 11, 2012, http://www.theatlantic.com/business/archive/2012/07/the-10-keys-to-building-the-flexible-workplace-of-the-future/259648/#.

8 Keith Hammonds, "Balance Is Bunk!" *Fast Company*, October 2004. http://www.fastcompany.com/51149/balance-bunk.

9 Matthew J. Grawitch et al., "Moving Toward a Better Understanding of the Work and Nonwork Interface," *Industrial and Organizational Psychology*, 4 (2011): 385–388.

10 "Personal Contact Preferred: Dealing with information overload, job satisfaction & mobility," *Randstad Workmonitor Global Press Report* (March 2012).

11 Cali Williams Yost, *Work+Life: Finding the Fit That's Right for You* (New York: Riverhead, 2005).

12 *2011 Work+Life Fit Reality Check*, Work+Life Fit, Inc., http://worklifefit.com/pr11a/wp-content/uploads/wlf_2011realitycheck_summary FINAL.pdf.

13 Lisa Belkin, "The Opt-Out Revolution," *New York Times*, October 23, 2003.

14 *Work+Life Fit blog*, http://worklifefit.com/blog/.

15 "Cali Williams Yost News Feed," *Fast Company*, http://www.fastcompany.com/user/cali-yost.

16 "Cali Williams Yost Forbes Blogs," *Forbes*, http://blogs.forbes.com/people/caliyost/.

17 Caroline Howard, "Top 100 Websites for Women 2012," *Forbes*, June 20, 2012. http://www.forbes.com/sites/forbeswomanfiles/2012/06/20/top-100-websites-for-women-2012/.

Chapter 1

1 Susan Gregory Thomas, "Are Dads the New Moms?" *Wall Street Journal*, May 11, 2012. http://online.wsj.com/article/SB10001424052702304 451104577392261536405038.html.

2 Carol Evans, "Are You Surprised Women Need To Thank Male Managers?" *Forbes*, February 23, 2012. http://www.forbes.com/sites/womensmedia/2012/02/23/are-you-surprised-women-need-to-thank-male-managers/.

3 Kerstin Aumann, Ellen Galinsky, and Kenneth Matos, "The New Male Mystique," Families and Work Institute, (2011).

4 Brad Harrington, Fred Van Deusen, and Beth Humberd, "The New Dad: Caring, Committed and Conflicted," Boston College (2011).

5 Shelley J. Correll, Stephen Benard, and In Paik, "Getting a Job: Is There a Motherhood Penalty?" *American Journal of Sociology*, Vol. 112, No. 5 (March, 2007): 1297–1339.

6 Dina Bakst, Jared Make, and Nancy Rankin, "Beyond the Breadwinner: Professional Dads Speak Out on Work and Family," A Better Balance (June 2011).

7 Aumann et al., "The New Male Mystique."

8 *2006 Work+Life Fit Reality Check*, Work+Life Fit, Inc., http://worklifefit. com/pdf/wlf_120706release4.pdf.

9 Peter Linkow, Jan Civian, and Kathleen M. Lingle, "Men and Work-Life Integration: A Global Study," WFD Consulting and WorldatWork's Alliance for Work-Life Progress (May 2011).

10 "Where Do College Grads Want to Work," Mashable.com, May 15, 2012. http://mashable.com/2012/05/15/top-jobs-college-grads/.

11 Stephanie Buck, "Managing Millennials: Why Gen Y Will Be Running the Country by 2020," *Mashable.com*, June 28, 2012. http://mashable .com/2012/06/28/millennials-work-jobs/.

12 *Caregiving in the U.S. 2009*, National Alliance for Caregiving and AARP (2009): 4.

13 *The Study of Caregiving Cost to Working Caregivers: Double Jeopardy of Baby Boomers Caring for Their Parents*, MetLife Mature Market Institute (June 2011).

14 Joshua M. Wiener and Jane Tilly, "Population Aging in the United States of America: Implications for Public Progammes," *International Journal of Epidemiology*, 31 (2002): 776–781.

15 Marci Alboher, "Eldercare, an Inevitable Work/Life Issue," *New York Times*, December 3, 2007. http://shiftingcareers.blogs.nytimes .com/2007/12/03/eldercare-an-inevitable-worklife-issue/.

16 Stephen Miller, "Baby Boomers Will Transform Aging, Work, and Retirement," *WeKnowNext.com*, May, 19, 2011. http://www.weknownext.com/ workforce/baby-boomers-will-transform-aging-work-and-retirement.

17 Marc Freedman, *The Big Shift: Navigating the New Stage Beyond Midlife* (New York: Public Affairs, 2011).

18 Dan Kadlec, "What Older Workers Want," *Time*, June 27, 2012. http:// moneyland.time.com/2012/06/27/what-older-workers-want/.

19 "Work & Retirement," AARP.com, http://www.aarp.org/work/.

Chapter 2

1 Bill Gross, "America's Debt is Not Its Biggest Problem," *Washington Post*, August 10, 2011, http://www.washingtonpost.com/opinions/ameri cas-debt-is-not-its-biggest-problem/2011/08/10/gIQAgYvE7I_story.html.

2 Kathy Gurchiek, "Job Security, Company Stability are Most Important, Generations Agree," *WeKnowNext.com*, September 15, 2011, http://www.weknownext.com/workplace/job-security-company-stability-are-most-important-generations-agree.

3 Glen E. Kreiner, Elaine C. Hollensbe, and Mathew L. Sheep, "Balancing Borders and Bridges: Negotiating the Work-Home Interface Via Boundary Work Tactics," *Academy of Management Journal* (2009): 704–730.

4 Matthew J. Grawitch, Larissa K. Barber, and Logan Justice, "Rethinking the Work-Life Interface: It's Not About Balance, It's About Resource Allocation," *Applied Psychology: Health and Well-Being* (2010): 127–159.

5 "When Work Works: Flex at a Glance," http://whenworkworks.org/research/downloads/FlexAtAGlance.pdf.

6 Maggie Jackson, *Distracted: The Erosion of Attention and the Coming Dark Age* (New York: Prometheus Books, 2009).

7 YoungAh Park and Steve M. Jex, "Work-Home Boundary Management Using Communication and Information Technology," *International Journal of Stress Management*, Vol. 18 (2011): 133–152.

Chapter 4

1 Cali Williams Yost, "Escape the 10 Tyrannies of Work/Life Balance," *Fast Company*, January 12, 2011. http://www.fastcompany.com/1716044/escape-10-tyrannies-work-life-balance.

2 Laura Vanderkam, *168 Hours: You Have More Time Than You Think*, (New York: Portfolio, 2010).

3 Tony Schwartz and Catherine McCarthy, "Manage Your Energy, Not Your Time," *Harvard Business Review* (October 2007).

4 "A Brief History of Time Management," *Inc*, http://www.inc.com/ss/
brief-history-time-management#1.

5 Geneen Roth, *Women Food and God: An Unexpected Path to Almost
Everything* (New York: Scribner, 2011).

Chapter 5

1 *2011 Work+Life Fit Reality Check*, Work+Life Fit, Inc., http://worklif
efit.com/pr11a/wp-content/uploads/wlf_2011realitycheck_summary
FINAL.pdf.

2 Ibid.

Chapter 11

1 "Overweight and Obesity," Centers for Disease Control and Prevention, http://www.cdc.gov/obesity/data/.

2 "Sleep Aids and Insomnia," National Sleep Foundation, http://www
.sleepfoundation.org/article/sleep-related-problems/sleep-aids-and
-insomnia.

3 Daniel Smith, "It's Still the 'Age of Anxiety.' Or Is It?" *New York Times*,
January 14, 2012, http://opinionator.blogs.nytimes.com/2012/01/14/its
-still-the-age-of-anxiety-or-is-it/.

4 "Attitudes and Impacts of Technology," Networked Workers--Pew Internet (2008), http://www.pewinternet.org/Reports/2008/Networked
-Workers/6-Attitudes-and-Impacts-of-Technology.aspx?view=all.

5 Annalyn Censky, "Vacation? No Thanks, Boss," *Money*, May 18, 2012,
http://money.cnn.com/2012/05/18/news/economy/unused_vacation
_days/index.htm.

Acknowledgments

Tweak It represents the collective wisdom of those I've worked with, lived with, and served over the past seventeen years to transform work and life and bring it into the twenty-first century. Your names could fill an entire chapter and more. You've allowed me to do the work I love and have the life I cherish, which can be especially challenging when you are writing a book and running a business while caring for yourself, your family, and friends. Thank you, all.

However, I want to give special recognition to the individuals directly responsible for helping me bring *Tweak It* into existence. First, thank you to my agent, Josh Getzler, and his assistant, Maddie Raffel. An author couldn't ask for a savvier partner and friend to join her on the publishing journey.

Many thanks to the entire team at Center Street/Hachette for their enthusiastic support of *Tweak It*. Senior Editor Kate Hartson, I am grateful that you said yes and for your ninjalike editorial insights. Associate Publisher Harry Helm, Director of Publicity Shanon Stowe, and Web Publicist Sarah Reck, thank you for your commitment to spread the *Tweak It* message as far and wide as possible.

As *Tweak It* began to emerge over the last few years, a number of people played particularly pivotal roles and should be recognized:

My friend and colleague, Maryella Gockel, who remarked one day as I shared book ideas over lunch, "I wish you would write a book about everyone's everyday work and life." She was right.

At a particularly frustrating point in the book-writing process, my friend CV Harquail said, "You should talk to Mark Levy." She's super smart, so I did. It was a turning point.

Mark Levy, what can I say? You are a master at unlocking the message. You are a magician, literally and figuratively.

Marci Alboher, thank you for your encouragement and willingness to share not only your encore career wisdom as one of the *Tweak It* Inspiration Experts, but for tapping your powerful network of contacts at the exact right time.

Julie Burstein and Jolie Solomon, who facilitated the Raise Our Voices program for the OpEd Project: you, along with the other members of our intrepid group, showed me how to unlock the power of my story and the stories of all the people I've met and worked with over the years.

To Deb Stier, Pam Kassner, MaryLea Crawley, and Joe Katz, thank you for feedback at key moments that sent me in the right direction.

To my Flex+Strategy Group/Work+Life Fit team: Donna Miller, Joanne Spigner, Janice Maffei, Lauren Fosbenner, and Linda Cannilla, thank you for your passionate commitment to our work and for your invaluable contributions to *Tweak It*. I marvel at your ability to bring vision to life.

And to the hundreds of organizations and tens of thousands of individuals who have shared their work+life fit and flexibility stories and goals with us over the years, it has been a privilege to support you. My favorite part of my job is working side by side with groups of committed leaders, managers, and employees to make work flexibility a strategic reality that benefits the business and its people.

I've saved the best for last. To my husband, Andy Yost, how did I ever get so lucky? For the past twenty-five years, I've thanked the universe daily for your love and support. Emma and Maddie, my smart, bright, loving, beautiful girls, there are no words to adequately describe how much your mama adores you.

As every parent knows, reliable, quality child care is a must. For the past ten years, Marcelina DosSantos has loved my children like her own. This has given me the gift to work without worry.

Finally, to my wonderful family and friends, especially Barbara Hughes and my lifelong college sister-friends, you give life true meaning. For your undying enthusiastic encouragement (and laughter!), I am forever grateful.

About Cali Williams Yost

When the C-Suite wants to make flexible work part of its organization's business strategy, executives call CALI WILLIAMS YOST, the CEO and Founder of the Flex+Strategy Group/Work+Life Fit™, Inc. For seventeen years, she has shown hundreds of organizations such as BDO USA, Pearson, Novo Nordisk, and the United Nations, as well as tens of thousands of individuals, how to partner for award-winning flexible work, and life, success.

Called "one of the smartest" and "sophisticated thinkers" by the *New York Times*, Cali Williams Yost has shaped the global dialogue on work+life flexibility for nearly two decades.

A former commercial banker and honors graduate of Columbia Business School, Yost is author of the critically acclaimed *Work+Life: Finding the Fit That's Right for You* (Riverhead/Penguin Group, 2005), the first guide to help people formally reset their work+life fit in response to a major life transition.

Since 2007, she has served as an expert contributor to Fast Company .com. And every year, from 2010 to 2012, Yost's Work+Life Fit Blog has been voted one of the Top 100 Websites for Women by Forbes.com.

An in-demand consultant, keynote speaker, and workshop presenter, Yost serves as an evangelist for the broad organizational impacts of work and life flexibility—from employee engagement, innovation, cost containment, and talent management to global client service, sustainability, and disaster preparedness. Her unique, often contrarian perspective has been featured in numerous national media outlets such as the *New York Times*, the *Wall Street Journal*, *BusinessWeek*, *Newsweek*, *USA Today*, NPR, and Fox Business News.

Prior to founding the Flex+Strategy Group/Work+Life Fit, Inc., Yost held senior consulting roles with the Families and Work Institute and Bright Horizons Family Solutions, two of the field's pioneering organizations. Yost lives in New Jersey with her husband and two daughters.